Children
OF THE
Movement

The sons and daughters of Martin Luther
King Jr., Malcolm X, Elijah Muhammad,
George Wallace, Andrew Young, Julian
Bond, Stokely Carmichael, Bob Moses,
James Chaney, Elaine Brown, and others
reveal how the civil rights movement
tested and transformed their families

John Blake

D0877866

Lawrence Hill Books

Library of Congress Cataloging-in-Publication Data

Blake, John.
Children of the movement : the sons and daughters of Martin Luther King, Jr.,
Malcolm X, Elijah Muhammad, George Wallace, Andrew Young, Julian Bond,
Stokely Carmichael, Bob Moses, James Chaney, Elaine Brown, and others reveal
how the civil rights movement tested and transformed their families / John
Blake.— 1st ed.
        p.   cm.
     ISBN 1-55652-537-0 (cloth)
     ISBN 1-55652-678-4 (paper)
     1. African American civil rights workers—Biography.   2. Civil
rights workers—United States—Biography.   3. Sons—United States—
Biography.   4. Daughters—United States—Biography.   5. African
American families.   6. Family—United States.   7. African
Americans—Civil rights—History—20th century.   8. Civil rights
movements—United States—History—20th century.   9. United
States—Race relations.   10. Southern States—Race relations.
I. Title.

E185.96.B5645   2004
323'.092'396073—dc22   2003027680

For TL

Cover art: ©Take Stock
Jacket design: Joan Sommers Design
Interior design: Pamela Juárez

First edition
Published by Lawrence Hill Books
An imprint of Chicago Review Press, Incorporated
814 North Franklin Street
Chicago, Illinois 60610
ISBN-13: 978-1-55652-678-7
ISBN-10: 1-55652-678-4
Printed in the United States of America
5 4 3 2 1

Contents

Acknowledgments

WRITING MY FIRST BOOK WAS BOTH an exhilarating and exhausting experience. But the task was made easier by so many people who helped and inspired me along the way. I want to first thank "Aunt Sylvia," my lifeline and inspiration. My agent, Pamela Harty, for her enthusiasm and support. Yuval Taylor, my editor, who showed a tremendous amount of faith and patience in me. My journalism mentors, Leon Carter and the late Jim Gallagher of the *Chicago Tribune*. My best friend, brother, and confidant, Patrick Blake. My cousin, Carolyn Forest, for her sage advice. My oldest brother, Twiggy. Juan Alberto and Erenie Hudson Pons, the gold standard.

Thanks to all the children of the movement and their parents who took time out of their busy lives to trust me with their memories.

And finally to Him: John 12:32.

Introduction

LIKE MOST AMERICANS I was conditioned to think about the civil rights movement in the past tense. The typical images that I saw from the movement—the black-and-white newsreels of King's "I Have a Dream" speech, police dogs attacking demonstrators, and protestors singing freedom songs—seemed to belong to another generation.

But one day I discovered that the drama of the movement wasn't confined to the past. It was still unfolding in the lives of a group of people seldom mentioned in the history books—the children of the movement's leading figures.

My discovery came during a phone call. I work as a journalist in Atlanta, the cradle of the civil rights movement, the birthplace of Dr. Martin Luther King Jr., and still the home of many movement leaders. Over the years, I had covered innumerable civil rights commemorative events; it's virtually a second industry in Atlanta. They all seemed to follow the same script: movement veterans being honored, speeches warning that the movement isn't over, and everybody grabbing hands to sing "We Shall Overcome." The events were supposed to be inspiring but they seemed prerecorded. I saw nothing of my generation in them. I heard nothing but platitudes about civil rights leaders. I started leaving the events early when the time came to sing. No one seemed to be saying anything new.

One afternoon I received a call from a publicist pitching a potential news story. During our conversation, she mentioned that she was the daughter of a famous civil rights leader. Expecting more platitudes, I asked her what her father was like. Instead I got pain. She gave me "Daddy Dearest" with a civil rights backdrop. At that moment I realized there was another way to look at these movement legends: through the eyes and lives of their children.

Questions began to come to me. What is it like to be the daughter of segregationist George Wallace? How do you deal with the expectations of being the child of Martin Luther King Jr., Stokely Carmichael, or Malcolm X? And what is it like to be the daughter of James Earl Chaney, one of three civil rights workers killed in that notorious Mississippi summer of 1964, when you were born only a week after he was murdered?

The answers to those questions provide the core of this book. For two years I spoke with the children of the most recognizable members in the movement, figuring they would offer the most dramatic stories. I plucked most of the names that popped up in civil rights documentaries and history books. But along the way, I broadened my search to include the children of segregationist leaders and civil rights martyrs, those ordinary activists whose murders triggered worldwide notoriety. And, whenever possible, I talked to the parents. I wanted to know about their relationship not just to their children, but also to their past. If they had it to do over, would they do anything differently? Do they still believe that "We Shall Overcome"?

Finally, I talked to the children of civil rights veterans who are now leaders in another exciting mass movement. These global justice protestors burst into most Americans' consciousness during the Seattle World Trade Organization (WTO) protests in 1999. Civil rights veterans insist that they've inspired all sorts of contemporary movements. These global justice activists represent the most dramatic example of this belief.

———— ❧ ————

Selecting the children I wanted to talk to was easy. I first called those children I thought would carry the heaviest burden from their last name. These were children such as Martin Luther King III and Andrew "Bo" Young III—people who had been named after their famous fathers and went on to choose similar careers. I also chose others, such as Ralph David Abernathy III, because they had become such controversial public figures. Finally, I talked to a third group, one that includes the daughter of James Earl Chaney, because most people don't even know they exist.

Getting some of these children to talk, though, was more difficult. Several flatly refused because they were trying to escape their parent's shadow. One, the eldest daughter of Malcolm X, wouldn't talk without being paid. Yet the majority seemed to relish the opportunity. It seemed like therapy to them. People like Bokar Ture, the son of Stokely Carmichael, are still figuring out what it means to be the son of a civil rights icon.

Despite the variety of movement children I talked to, certain themes did emerge. A large number of them are emotionally distant from their parents who, they say, are more suited for protest than parenthood. Some seem to have no idea how famous their parents were or how much they suffered. And, surprisingly, many are more pessimistic than their parents about improving society. They saw their parents' idealism chewed up by the movement. They're not going to try to change the world.

Yet some have made inspiring changes in their own lives. The daughter of a notoriously racist Southern governor found her calling as a teacher in an all-black inner-city school. The young son of a famous black nationalist talks with awe about the selflessness of his father—never seeming to notice that he himself is displaying those same qualities in his own life. And the daughter of one of the movement's most famous martyrs talks about an unexpected meeting with her mother's killer that tested her capacity for forgiveness.

As we move forward through a new century, the movement is in danger of being obscured by sentimentality. The movement's triumphs are now talked about as if they were inevitable and every politician seems to claim that he or she once marched with Martin Luther King.

But we forget how brutal it was. The movement's aftershocks continue to ripple through the lives of its veterans and their children—just as its political implications continue to ignite freedom struggles around the world. What happened back then shapes all of our lives today—even the lives of those who dismiss that era.

In a sense, we are all children of the movement.

1

Casualties of War

THE CIVIL RIGHTS MOVEMENT now occupies a cozy place in America's collective memory.

Schoolchildren dutifully learn about Rosa Parks refusing to give up her bus seat. Civil rights battlegrounds in places like Selma, Alabama, have been turned into tourist stops. Every January, politicians and aging civil rights veterans solemnly gather in front of cameras to commemorate the birthday of Martin Luther King Jr.

The platitudes about the movement have become so ingrained in our daily lives that it's easy to forget the desperation that inspired the civil rights struggle. It wasn't just a movement; it was a war. Activists were tortured in jail, beaten by mobs, ostracized by their families. People were murdered.

Some never recovered physically or psychologically from their experiences, says Taylor Branch, the Pulitzer Prize–winning author of *Parting the Waters*. "They became casualties of war. It was a war in which they were spectacularly triumphant, but they were treated and ignored like it was a war that they lost."

Several of these casualties passed their wounds on. Their pain prevented them from becoming close to their children.

Reverend James Bevel, part of Martin Luther King's inner circle, is no longer on speaking terms with two of his daughters. Others simply kept their grief to themselves. James Forman Sr., former executive director of Student Nonviolent Coordinating Committee (SNCC), never seemed to know how to speak to his two sons about the trauma he experienced in Mississippi. The daughter of James Zwerg, a Freedom Rider, first learned about the magnitude of her father's suffering from a history textbook.

It was strange to talk to these movement veterans about their personal struggles with their children. When we discussed the politics of the movement, they would effortlessly and eloquently riff about nonviolence and social change. But when I started asking simple questions about their feelings for their children, some would suddenly stop and grasp for words. Their children, however, had plenty to say.

———∞∞∞———

Chevara Orrin and Bacardi Jackson
Daughters of the Rev. James Bevel

CHEVARA SLAMMED ON HER BRAKES and swerved onto the shoulder of an Atlanta freeway when she heard the radio announcement. Reverend James Bevel, a civil rights activist, was speaking that night in an Atlanta church. She reversed directions and drove there. When she entered the crowded sanctuary, she sat in the front row and locked eyes with Bevel before he rose to speak.

Bevel was accustomed to being center stage. He was a leader in the student sit-in movement during the early 1960s and part of Martin Luther King Jr.'s inner circle. He was one of King's best tacticians, the man whose organizing ability helped give the movement many of its most inspiring victories.

That evening Bevel began preaching a sermon on the Old Testament hero Noah. But suddenly he went off onto another subject—the evils of white people. He compared white people to maggots and declared that white women were only good for use as sex pets or slaves—all the while looking at Chevara in the front row.

Chevara bolted from her chair in the middle of the sermon and fled to a bathroom where she sobbed. There was a lifetime of hurt behind her tears. Bevel is her father, the one-time companion of her white Jewish mother.

Chevara, a caramel-colored thirty-six-year-old woman with high cheekbones, bears a striking resemblance to Bevel. Years after the incident at that Atlanta church, her voice still rises in anger when she recalls the moment. "He was negating my very existence," she says. "I wanted to stand up and shout to him, 'How dare you? Here I am your own daughter, the result of a relationship between you and a white woman.' I was just devastated."

Bevel is a legend among students of the civil rights movement. But he's no hero to Chevara or to her sister, Bacardi. Both say their father never provided for them while they endured a childhood marked by homelessness, welfare, and hand-me-down clothes. He was too preoccupied with his place in the movement to notice them. "He doesn't know my favorite food," Chevara says. "He doesn't know where I went to high school. He doesn't know what my college degree is in. He doesn't even know when I was born."

I meet the sisters in the suburban Atlanta home they share. As I talk to them about their father, their moods alternate between anger and laughter as they recount the exchanges they've had with him. "He's great in many ways and he's done some great things," thirty-three-year-old Bacardi says. "But he's always failed miserably as a father."

Bevel, sixty-seven, now lives in Chicago. He doesn't apologize for his absence. He says the movement was all-consuming. Sacrifices had to be made. His daughters could have seen him more if they had decided to become activists like him. "They don't understand my vocation. My vocation is to deal with the salvation, education, and liberation of American people. That's all I worked on. Apart from this, I don't exist. In order to be with me, you have to work on this."

Bevel's dedication as a parent may be questioned, but not his place in civil rights history. He is best known today for his role in the 1963 campaign to desegregate Birmingham, which was then considered the South's most segregated city. The campaign had stalled because Martin Luther King Jr. had run out of demonstrators willing to fill the jails. Bevel proposed a daring move: use children as demonstrators. He persuaded King to accept his strategy, over great opposition from King's advisors.

The audacious move, which some dubbed "the Children's Miracle," became a movement turning point. The images of Birmingham's public safety commissioner, Eugene "Bull" Connor, turning fire hoses and attack dogs against child demonstrators gained international sympathy for the movement. Birmingham's white business leaders agreed to desegregate the city.

Chevara Orrin, left, and younger sister Bacardi Jackson pose in the backyard of their Atlanta home.

Thrust onto the public stage, Bevel became one of the movement's most colorful characters. With his volcanic sermons and the Jewish skullcap and overalls that were his uniform, he was known as one of King's "crazy people"—the ones pushing the movement to go in bold directions.

"He's like an Old Testament prophet," Taylor Branch says. "He hears voices. Sometimes they are the voices of genius and sometimes they are the voices of lunacy."

Bevel's eccentric nature seemed pathological at times, says John Lewis, a friend of Bevel's from the sit-in movement and now a Georgia state representative. He says the Southern Christian Leadership Conference (SCLC) banned Bevel after he once locked himself into a hotel room with a group of college coeds, declared himself a prophet, urinated in a glass, and ordered them to drink its contents to prove their loyalty.

Like other movement activists, Bevel appeared to have lost his way after King was killed, Lewis says. "Bevel had so much hope, so much optimism. I think it was too much for him and many others when King died."

Susanne Jackson, a rumpled, heavyset woman with a wary manner, met Bevel in 1965 when he came to Chicago to join the SCLC's campaign for open housing. Jackson was an antiwar activist, and as Bevel moved into antiwar protesting, they began an on-again, off-again six-year relationship.

Jackson says she was impressed by Bevel's intelligence and charisma. She liked the way he treated women. "He would listen to women and utilize their ideas, which was not typical of many of the movement's leaders of the time. He could be intense about understanding you and zeroing in on where you were coming from."

Four years into their relationship, Jackson gave birth to Chevara; two years later she had Bacardi. Chevara was named after the popular 1960s revolutionary, Che Guevara. Bacardi, born on New Year's Eve, was named after the rum favored by holiday revelers.

Those names weren't traditional, but neither was Jackson's relationship with Bevel. Like many 1960s activists, by forging an interracial relationship they were challenging not only the era's notion of race, but also its rules about raising children.

The daughters called their parents by their first names. They lived alternately on a communal farm and in a communal home with Black Panther Party members. Their home life was unstable. They only lived briefly with Bevel. He didn't hold a steady job and was often away taking part in demonstrations. Jackson decided her daughters would have more stability if she raised them alone.

She moved to Memphis and took jobs with the National Urban League and the city's black newspaper. But income from those jobs wasn't enough. She eventually had to go on welfare to support her daughters, who sometimes had nothing to eat but farina, peanut butter sandwiches, and powdered milk.

Courtesy of AP/Wide World Photos

Reverend James Bevel, with his trademark skullcap, delivers a sermon in the early 1960s. His ability to rally youth would prove crucial in the 1963 Birmingham campaign, but he had far more trouble relating to his daughters.

Bevel wasn't with them during their struggles. They say he rarely visited. He never attended any of their birthday parties. He didn't attend their graduations. He rarely called.

Bacardi's first memory of her father dates from the age of five, when he took her to a meeting of movement veterans at the Lorraine Motel in Memphis (the place where King was assassinated). "He seemed like he was important," she says. "People knew who he was and they said he had done something great."

When Bacardi was ten, Bevel came to Memphis for a visit. She says he showed no interest in her personal life. Instead he would lecture her about his greatness, comparing himself to Jesus and Zeus. "I didn't like him at all. He talked about how great he was. He was trying to come in and impart wisdom. But for me, it was like, 'Who are you to come in and tell us anything? You don't know me.'"

At the same time, Bacardi developed a grudging respect for her father after hearing him speak. "He's a very charismatic man," she says. "People are really impressed when they hear him speak. He can silence a room."

Bevel's daughters didn't have much opportunity to witness that charisma firsthand. They say they saw their father on only three extended occasions during their entire childhood.

Jackson would plead with Bevel to visit their daughters, but he was too wrapped up in the movement. "I would tell him, 'you should talk to your children,'" she says. "He would not disagree but he would say it wasn't feasible."

Jackson didn't consider taking Bevel to court for child support when her daughters were still minors. She feared the news that Bevel was in an interracial relationship would limit his effectiveness as a movement leader. "At that point in time, it would have been a major civil rights issue because of race and everything related to it. I didn't think that would be appropriate. And I wasn't sure I was going to be believed."

The sisters began to attend public school in inner-city Memphis during the 1970s. Both faced pressure from an unexpected front: they were teased by black kids for having a white mother.

Chevara says her mother was treated worse. She was often called "honky," "white trash," or "bitch" by blacks in public. Some even threw bottles and cans at her mother—sometimes when she and her sister were present—as they drove by in cars.

The taunts didn't drive a wedge in the family, each member says today. The sisters say their mother became their hero. She took them to countless marches and city council meetings. She gave them hand-made black history books, books she copied by hand after borrowing them from the library because she couldn't afford to buy them.

"Everything that I know about the struggle—not just the civil rights movement, but the human rights movement, about economic issues, women's issues—all those are because of Sue," says Chevara.

Both daughters went to college on full scholarships. Chevara graduated from the University of Memphis, Bacardi from Stanford University and Yale Law School. Today, Chevara, a publicist who also volunteers at two child abuse prevention organizations, lives in Atlanta with her husband and two sons. Bacardi is an attorney for King & Spalding, one of Atlanta's top law firms.

When the two sisters became adults, they decided to seek out their father. Bevel had faded from public view, emerging only to attend civil rights commemorative events. By the 1990s, though, Bevel was back in the news. In 1992 he became the vice presidential running mate of Lyndon LaRouche, a maverick politician. In 1994 he allied himself with another controversial figure, Louis Farrakhan. He began writing a column for the Nation of Islam's *Final Call* newspaper. A year later, he persuaded Farrakhan to hold the Million Man March on Washington.

It was then that Chevara made her first attempt to contact her father. When she heard over an Atlanta radio station that her father was going to speak at an Atlanta church, she drove there hoping for reconciliation.

But she never had the talk with her father she intended. She became so angry when her father attacked white women from the pulpit that she left the church in tears. When she called her father later that night to ask about his comments, he attributed his remarks to his alliance with Farrakhan.

Bacardi contacted her father the same year, sending a four-page typed letter to him from Yale.

The letter veered from bitterness and sadness to a matter-of-fact summary of her life. She greeted him with "Daddy Dearest." "I also have no illusions that as much as I long to have a real father," she wrote, "a million lies would never transform you into one."

Still, a tentative dialogue followed between Bacardi and her father. They spoke by phone. He visited her briefly in Atlanta.

But Bacardi says her father would never apologize for his absence. In one of the last letters she received from him when she was in college, Bevel acknowledged that the wall that separates him and his

James Bevel, now wearing a beret instead of a skullcap, standing outside his Chicago office in 2000. He doesn't understand his daughter's bitterness toward him.

daughters may never be removed, but that distance could not be his major concern. He loved her, he said, but only "as I do all people, and I will work for your health, interest, rights, and needs as I do for all people. . . ."

Bevel then scolded his daughter for her political apathy. He told her that when he was her age, he didn't pursue personal success like she did because he chose to fight against segregation. He ended the letter by saying that he could "no longer look for my children to work for the liberation of our people."

Bacardi abandoned her attempt to reconcile with her father. "He speaks in political theory all the time," she says, shaking her head. "He is never out of that mode."

Bacardi and Chevara discovered something else about their father. Whenever they attended various civil rights movement commemorative events, they ran into people who said that they too were Bevel's children. These meetings became so common that Chevara and Bacardi organized a meeting of the people who claimed to be Bevel's children. After comparing notes and talking to extended family, the daughters estimate that their father has at least seventeen children.

After talking to his daughters in Atlanta, I fly to Chicago to meet Bevel. He owns a dry-cleaning shop today. He says he's still fighting for social progress. He runs a program to help at-risk youth and teaches effective parenting. Bevel runs both his business and his program out of a dilapidated building in a rundown part of Chicago's South Side next to railroad tracks, a check-cashing business, and a sub shop. The wail of police sirens and train whistles constantly fills the air.

Bevel greets me warily, looking me up and down for a moment without saying anything. He still dresses as if he's on the frontlines of Birmingham: black beret, overalls, and sandals. He carries a battered briefcase, which contains yellowed news clippings and history books in which he's underlined the passages written about him.

When I start to ask Bevel about his daughters, he shrugs me off. He doesn't want to talk about his personal life. He prefers politics. While his thirty-three-year-old wife, Erika, takes notes, Bevel jumps before a blackboard and furiously starts drawing diagrams to explain his political philosophy.

After hearing his political views, I insist on asking questions about his daughters. "How many children do you have?" I inquire.

"Well, the computer broke down," he says, smiling. "I don't get into counting things like that."

"Do you believe that you were a good father to your daughters?"

"I'm in America as a father for all black children," he says, anger now creeping into his voice.

"Did you ever refer to white women as sex pets and toys?"

"I don't know," he says. Then he draws another diagram on the board and starts to talk about the evils of segregation.

Trying to get Bevel to answer a question is like trying to catch a fly. His conversation follows no discernable pattern. He bounces from lectures on nonviolent social change to suddenly talking about sex, prostitution, and pimps. He meets every question about his relationship to his daughters by citing his activism.

Finally he starts to talk more about his daughters. He says that he couldn't provide income to his children because he had no steady job. He was an activist who lived off of the goodwill of the people he served. Besides, he added, if his children were hungry at any time, they could have received food by simply going to various preachers in Memphis who would have been happy to feed Jim Bevel's daughters.

Bevel says he gave his daughters something more precious than a meal. He helped them win the right to vote. "Look, if you and twenty million folks couldn't vote and a preacher came along and got you the right to vote, how much tithe do you owe him?" he asks me.

I then ask him if that means then that his daughters actually owe him.

"You damn right!"

Bevel then smiles and says he is not dismayed by his daughters' animosity toward him. "Bull Connor hated me, but I loved him."

––––––––—∞∞∞—––––––––

Today, Bevel and his daughters rarely talk. When Chevara occasionally calls him, he asks if she is ever going to join his movement. She's no longer trying to reconcile with him. "I don't see that the responsibility should be on me to forge a relationship with him," she says. "I don't think that's the child's responsibility. I don't care how old the child gets."

Bacardi has stopped trying to understand her father. She no longer writes him. She says she is finding solace from her childhood void in a newfound commitment to her church. Her Christian faith tells her that she should forgive her father, but she struggles with that challenge. "He's never said he was sorry once," she says. "He's told a million black men that they need to atone and take responsibility for their families, but he hasn't done either in his personal life."

She even wonders how her relationship with her father has shaped her own personality. "It's been an obvious gap in my existence, to not have somebody from whom you can measure what manhood should be about," she says. "To not have someone there who could protect us against the world. That caused me to grow up with a lot of insecurities."

Chevara doesn't see the need to forgive her father. There are two Jim Bevels for her. There is the one in the history books, the one whose leadership opened doors for her generation. Then there is her father. He closed the door on her childhood.

One day Chevara shows me a history book with a photo of her father in his youth. In it, Bevel rallies demonstrators from behind a pulpit in Birmingham, jabbing his preaching finger in the air. A smile crosses her face as she points out passages about him. She seems proud of his work in the movement. As I look at the picture in the book and at her, I tell her that she looks like her father's twin: the same high cheekbones and complexion. She even has the same rapid-fire manner of speech.

Chevara's face clouds. The smile is gone.

"I'm always struck by how much I look like him," she finally says as she stares at the picture. "But it bothers me because I don't want the resemblance to be anything more than skin-deep."

Then her voice trails off and she closes the book. She turns and stares stone-faced into the distance as tears well up in her eyes.

Chaka Forman
Son of James Forman Sr.

CHAKA FORMAN IS A THIRTY-THREE-YEAR-OLD Hollywood actor who wonders if he chose the wrong part in life to play. He spends his days guest-starring on television shows, nabbing an occasional film role, and going to cattle-call auditions in which he has three minutes to convince a casting agent that he's the right man for the part.

It's not the life that his father wanted him to lead. James Forman, the former executive director of the Student Nonviolent Coordinating Committee (SNCC), led the group during one of its darkest periods, the Mississippi Freedom Summer. Three civil rights workers were murdered when groups of white Northern college students traveled South during the summer of 1964 to help local black activists register black voters. Chaka's mother is Constancia "Dinky" Romilly, a white civil rights activist.

"I often wonder if my parents are disappointed with the track I chose," he says. "We [he and his older brother, James Forman Jr.] were filled with this expectation to make the world a better place. There's not a day that goes by that I don't wonder if I'm wasting my time, if I'm not living up to my legacy."

Chaka's greatest performance, though, may be the one taking place offstage. He's been able to close some of the emotional distance between himself and his father. He refused to play the part of the bitter child.

While his father made his name during the movement, Chaka is making his on television. He won a part as one of three leads on *Hyperion Bay*, a television series that ran in 1998 and 1999. He's also had guest-starring roles on shows such as *Walker, Texas Ranger*; *CSI*; *NYPD Blue*; and *The Pretender*.

James Forman, fourth from left, leads the march from Atlanta University to the Georgia state capitol in 1966. Ralph David Abernathy is second from left. To Forman's immediate right is Coretta Scott King; next to her is Martin Luther King Jr., and on the far right is John Lewis.

As Chaka talks to me about his acting career from his Los Angeles home, it's easy to see why he would gravitate to the stage. He is a natural performer—funny, expressive, ebullient. His pride in his parents and his older brother, James, pours through his conversations.

Chaka says he's tried to balance his urge for social justice through nonacting jobs. In his spare time, he teaches Shakespeare to juvenile inmates at a maximum-security prison in Northern California. He's also earned teaching credentials as a special-education instructor and is an occasional substitute teacher.

He's discovered that helping others ended up helping him as an actor. "My auditions got better because I didn't care as much. Instead of going in—'I gotta get this job!'—I was like, 'Whatever. I know what I'm doing. I've already made a difference to thirty kids today. So when I walk into your room at four o'clock today, you can look at me however you want because I know who I am and what I got going on."

When Chaka managed to earn a little acting fame, two things happened to him: people started asking him for his autograph in public, and he started making a lot of money. "The more money you make, the more stuff you get free," he says, laughing. "Like shoes, jewelry, meals, clothes."

Yet Chaka's brief taste of Hollywood fame left him unfulfilled. Friends told him that he should run for the school board or city council. Others suggested that he could blend acting and activism as do Tim Robbins and Susan Sarandon, two of his career models.

Some of his friends have also tried to reassure him that he performs a community service just by allowing people to escape the demands of life through art. "But that's not enough for me," Chaka says. "I wonder how I can do what I love and still feel like I'm doing something for the community."

Courtesy of Chaka Forman

Chaka Forman with his father, James Forman, in the middle, and his brother, James Forman Jr., on the right.

Chaka's father tried to warn him that he would face that kind of dilemma. When he was acting on *Hyperion Bay*, his father told him that he was part of a capitalistic enterprise that exploited people. "And I'm like, 'I'm not exploiting anybody. I'm getting paid by Warner Bros.,'" Chaka says. "And he's like, 'Well, who are they exploiting?' We'd get into it. I love it. My dad will take you downtown."

Chaka's father made it clear to him what career he wanted Chaka to pursue. "He was so happy when I got my teaching credentials. When I'd call him, he'd ask what I did today. When I said, 'I taught,' he would say, 'That's great.' When I'd call again and he'd ask what I did today and I said I had an audition, he'd say, 'Oh, OK.'"

Ironically, Chaka says he initially decided to become an actor because of his father. He wanted to make enough money to help him. When he and his brother visited their father in Washington, D.C., he would become dismayed watching his father scratch out a living while staying in a small rented apartment with a black-and-white television set.

"We'd go to these civil rights functions and Marion Barry would be there, Julian Bond, John Lewis, and they all seemed to be in a much different financial place than my dad," Chaka says. "My brother would always talk about the sell-out mentality, where a lot of civil rights guys kind of cashed in on their notoriety, but my dad kept it real. He wasn't interested in that, in new suits or new things."

Whenever he brought these feelings up with his father, though, his father would maintain that he was just fine. "He was always selfless, whatever he needed to get by was fine with him. He talks to everybody on the street. On a daily basis he was out doing something to help somebody."

Chaka knew his father's selflessness had made him a leader in the movement, but he didn't realize how important his father was until he attended Brown University. It hit him when he saw his father's autobiography, *The Making of Black Revolutionaries*, on one of his class course reading lists.

There were other clues along the way. Once, when he was flying to Washington to visit his father, he was carrying a photo of his father marching with the writer James Baldwin and the singer Joan Baez in Selma in 1965. The photo had been reprinted in a history book and Chaka had blown up a copy for himself. "Three or four people in the airport stopped me and said, 'Hey, what do you have to do with this?'" he says. "When I told them he was my dad they would tell me he was such a powerhouse."

Yet even powerhouses need help. Chaka says his father has always been more comfortable talking about ideas than feelings. His father divorced his mother when he was a child, which added to the distance Chaka felt from him. (Both of Chaka's parents declined to talk with me about the reasons for their divorce.)

Chaka says his father is uncomfortable expressing his feelings because he had to keep a lid on them during the movement. "He lived in a time when you had to keep a lot of emotions in check if you're going to keep moving. You couldn't be worried about your friend dying and expressing your emotion if you were going to take another step forward." Forman witnessed some of the movement's most brutal episodes. He joined the Freedom Rides, on which groups of civil rights workers were savagely beaten by white mobs for trying to integrate interstate travel. Then three civil rights workers who worked under him were killed during Mississippi's Freedom Summer.

A native of Chicago, James Forman served in the Air Force during the Korean War and was a reporter for the *Chicago Defender* before joining SNCC. His maturity and range of experience led him to become SNCC's executive director in 1964.

James, Chaka's brother, is an attorney who cofounded a charter school in Washington for dropouts and youths who have been imprisoned. James also says he has trouble talking to his father. As a child, whenever James wanted to talk about himself, his father used the occasion to give him a lecture about some historical event or figure. "Sometimes when you're a kid, you're not really trying to talk to your parents and hear the encyclopedia version of what happened. I wanted to talk about what I was going through, not the Communist Party, Malcolm X, and the Nation of Islam. We talked much more about history than about me."

After a while, James says, he gave up trying to talk to his father about emotional issues. "To be honest, I don't ask him any question that needs to be answered within a minute."

But Chaka kept trying to break through to his father. When he was twenty years old, Chaka says he wrote his father an impassioned letter pleading for a closer relationship.

He mailed it immediately before he could change his mind and waited for a response. When he didn't receive one within a week, he called his father to ask him if he had received his letter. "I was expecting something big, and he said [he imitates his father's raspy, businesslike voice], 'Oh yeah, I got your letter. I appreciate it. You said a lot of important things, a lot of valid things. Love to come down and discuss them.'"

Chaka laughs at his father's response. "My letter was so emotional and he was clinical," Chaka says. "With my dad, he's lived so long alone; he's learned to shut out emotions."

Now Chaka is trying to bring his father and brother closer together. He says their relationship has long been strained, but it's improved over the last six years. "My brother and my dad are a lot alike in terms of not dealing with emotions. They put their work first. I put my emotions first. I always want to talk about how people feel. That's one of the reasons I became an actor—because I love the explorations of your soul. But they don't like to talk about how they feel. They're very scientific and analytical."

During visits to his father's Washington apartment, Chaka would try to persuade his father and brother to talk about their relationship. But both refused. "James would leave in a huff," he says. "Me and my dad would be sitting there in his little apartment and I'd be like, 'Dad, do you get lonely?' And he'd look at me like that was such a strange question."

Courtesy of Chaka Forman

Chaka Forman as a young boy laughs with his father, James Forman.

For the past thirteen years, Chaka's father has battled colon cancer. Chaka says he has tried to persuade his brother to visit his father more. His father, though ill, wouldn't ask his oldest son to spend more time with him. "My dad would say, 'Your brother is very busy,' and I'm like, 'Bullshit. He needs to be here with you.' I would really get angry about the fact they didn't see each other very often because I knew it would enrich their lives. I knew that they needed each other more than they wanted to admit."

Recently, however, Chaka says his brother has become closer to his father. James helps his father by running errands for him and spending time with him. According to Chaka, "He turned it around."

When asked about his brother's comments, a bemused smile crosses James's face. "Chaka has thought about these issues more than I have," James says. "He'd probably say I was stubborn like my dad." He doesn't agree with his brother's opinion that he is emotionally detached like his father. "I'm not mad at him for thinking that. I don't think it's a big deal. Chaka comes up with these analyses; he's like an armchair psychologist."

Instead, James offers another reason for the closer relationship he now enjoys with his father. "I just matured. I just realized what I had to do in the world. When you get older, you're less about what you want to do and more about what you're supposed to do."

I fly to Washington, D.C., to meet the elder Forman. The image I have of him is of the young, burly leader from Mississippi Freedom Summer. The man who emerges from a cab to meet me looks nothing like that. I'm shocked. For a moment, I mistake him for a homeless person.

Forman wears a dirty neck brace. An old baby-blue polyester suit is draped over his gaunt body. Age and his battle with cancer have literally bent his body like a sickle.

We talk in the auditorium of the charter school Forman Jr. runs. When I begin asking him about his relationship with his sons, he gets bewildered. He doesn't want to talk about them. He wants to talk about how his place in history has been ignored. "I think I should have a Nobel Peace Prize," he says. "The fact that I have not been awarded one is an example of the kind of racism in today's society."

Forman says that he also deserves more "remuneration" for his activism, just like many of his colleagues from the movement. "I didn't start off looking for money—man, I'm broke. I need some money. I'm not ashamed to say that to your readers."

When the subject of any emotional difficulties he may have had as a result of the movement comes up, Forman visibly bristles. He says he never suffered any emotional trauma from his days in the movement. He concedes, though, that he feels no nostalgia for that period in his life. "No, I'm glad it's over with. I don't grieve for it because it was a very painful period in history."

I ask Forman if his sons ever told him that it was difficult for them to deal with his absences during their childhood. (They were primarily raised by their mother.)

Chaka Forman in 1999, when he played Marcus Fox on the Warner Brothers television series *Hyperion Bay*.

"No, they did not—not that I know of," he says. "My answer to the question would be no. But we come from a split family. But why is the family split? That's a whole other question. I don't want to get involved in it."

I then ask Forman if he saw some of his personality traits in his eldest son, James.

"Well, I don't know what those things mean," he says. "I see in James a person who's trying very hard to build a better world. The same thing with Chaka. . . ."

Then, as if an invisible switch has been turned on, Forman abruptly changes the subject. He starts talking about how sad it is that Washington, D.C., hasn't yet achieved statehood. He goes into an extended riff on black history. The time for personal questions has come to an end. He asks if I would like to buy a copy of his autobiography.

His son Chaka, though, doesn't seem like he's going to have any problem expressing his feelings. He's full of ideas about his future. He's going to make a film about his father's life. He's going to write a script about his brother's charter school in Washington. Maybe he will run for public office one day. Meanwhile, he's going to try to make it in Los Angeles as an actor without losing the idealism instilled by his parents. "I've seen a lot of cats come out here and they get their soul sapped and drained out of them," he says. "That's not going to happen to me, not with my parents."

For the moment he's going to try everything he can to make sure that he doesn't settle into the role of the embittered movement kid longing for his father's affection. He's going to continue trying to bridge the distance between himself and his father, who has mystified his doctors by surviving colon cancer much longer than they expected. Chaka visits his father whenever he can, anxious as ever to share his feelings. "I sleep in my dad's house," Chaka says. "I spend twenty-four/seven with him. I'm quite honest with my feelings. It's a yearning, a need for affection, trying to make up for lost time."

Now Chaka says he is finally starting to win over his toughest audience: his father. "My dad tells me he loves me now," he says. "He didn't used to tell me that."

Mary Brown
Daughter of James Zwerg

THE MOB WAS ALREADY WAITING FOR JAMES ZWERG by the time the Greyhound bus eased into the bus station in Montgomery, Alabama.

Looking out the window, Zwerg could see men gripping baseball bats, chains, and clubs. They had sealed off the streets leading to the station and chased away news photographers. They didn't want anyone to witness what they were about to do.

Zwerg accepted his worst fear—he was going to die today.

Only the night before, Zwerg had prayed for the strength to not strike back in anger. He was among the eighteen white and black college students from Nashville, Tennessee, who had decided to take the Greyhound bus trip through the segregated South in 1961. They called themselves Freedom Riders. Their goal was to desegregate public transportation.

The Alabama bus ride was their first trip. Zwerg had not planned to go, but the night before some students had asked him to join them. To summon his courage, Zwerg stayed up late into the night, reading Psalm 27, the scripture that the students had picked to read during a group prayer before their trip.

"The Lord is my light and my salvation—of whom shall I fear?" the psalm began. But there was another passage at the end that touched Zwerg in a place the other students didn't know about: "Though my mother and father forsake me, the Lord will receive me."

Zwerg's parents had forsaken him for joining the civil rights movement. That same night, he had written a letter to his parents that was to be handed to them in case he was killed. The letter explained his decision to join the Freedom Riders.

Zwerg called his mother the night before he left to tell her where he was going.

"Don't go. Don't go," she said. "You can't do this to your father."

"I have no choice. I have to," he said.

"You killed your father," his mother replied. Then she hung up.

And now he was about to be killed. The Greyhound bus doors hissed open—Zwerg had volunteered to go first. The mob swarmed him as he stepped off the bus, yelling, "Nigger lover! Nigger lover!"

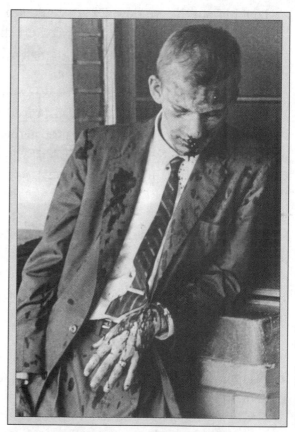

Courtesy of Bettman/Corbis

Then twenty-one years old, James Zwerg stands bleeding just after he was attacked by a white mob at a bus station in Montgomery, Alabama, in 1961. The infamous photo, which was published throughout the country, drove a wedge between Zwerg and his parents.

Then, as the mob grabbed him, Zwerg closed his eyes and bowed his head to pray. "The Lord is my light and salvation, of whom shall I fear. . . ."

The mob dragged him away.

What happened next would furnish the civil rights movement with one of its most unforgettable images. Photographers eventually broke through and snapped pictures of what the mob had done to James Zwerg and another Freedom Rider, John Lewis. The pictures were broadcast around the world.

Zwerg looked like a bloody scarecrow. His eyes were blackened and his suit was splattered with blood. After he was hospitalized, a news crew filmed him from his hospital bed. Barely able to speak, Zwerg nonetheless declared that violence wouldn't stop him or any of his friends. The Freedom Rides would go on.

Zwerg became one of the movement's first heroes. Although his physical wounds healed, the emotional ones took longer. He was wracked with guilt and depression after the beating. He drank too much, contemplated suicide, and finally had to seek therapy.

Zwerg's pain is something that is difficult for his daughter, Mary Brown, to understand. The distance she feels from her father isn't caused by her hurt or his unwillingness to share, but by her incomprehension. For much of her life, she didn't realize how scarring her father's experiences in the movement had been. He was simply her dad, not a civil rights symbol.

I talk to Mary, a thirty-four-year-old teacher, from her home in Tucson, Arizona. She is one of three children of Zwerg and his wife, Carolyn, who have been married for thirty-nine years.

Mary says the only time she ever saw her father cry was at her wedding. "Other than that, he really doesn't share a lot," she says. "I think he tries not to get too emotional."

Courtesy of Beloit College

James Zwerg speaking at a college in 2002 about his time as a Freedom Rider. Zwerg's story has been featured in several PBS specials.

She didn't even learn the full details about her father's role as a Freedom Rider until she was a sixteen-year-old high school student. Her social studies class was studying the civil rights movement when she told her teacher that her father was mentioned in the book *Eyes on the Prize*. The teacher asked Mary to bring the book in.

When she brought the book to class, she was shocked by her teacher's reaction. "It was the first time I'd ever heard my teacher swear. He said, 'Oh my God, you're dad's a fucking hero.' And I was like, 'What? He's just my dad.'"

The teacher then invited her father to speak to the class. When Zwerg accepted the invitation, Mary sat in class and listened along with her classmates as her father talked about his experiences with the mob. It was a revelation to her.

"That's when it really hit me that my dad was a big deal," she says. "I never took it all that seriously until then."

For Mary, the level of hate her father endured seems incomprehensible today. Her ex-husband is black and she has three biracial children. She's never had any problem going out in public with her husband or children. In fact, she's accustomed to strangers doting on her kids.

"When my oldest one was four years old, he asked me why his skin was darker," she says. "I explained to him that he was my little rainbow. He told me that he wanted to be like me but I kept on saying no, you're beautiful just like you are. He hasn't had any problems since then."

Brown lives in a mixed neighborhood with black, biracial, white, and Latino families. Color doesn't seem to matter, even when it comes to dating. "I've only dated black men," she says. "I really don't know why. Anytime I go out somewhere, black men would approach me before white men."

Given her own experience, Brown finds it inconceivable that her father was almost beaten to death just for riding a bus with civil rights activists. "It surprises me how much hate there was in the world," she says. "I don't see that now. I haven't experienced anything like what he went through."

While she was in high school, Mary says, her father began to share more of his feelings about his time as a civil rights activist. He had also helped integrate lunch counters. He showed her newspaper articles he had saved. But the gesture that affected her most was his sharing of excerpts from his college diary. "That is really what touched me," she says. "I didn't know—he doesn't talk about it to students—the fact that while he would stand in line somebody would spit on him or hit him in the head with a brick."

⸻ ❧ ⸻

Zwerg's daughter has a hard time understanding what her father did; but his parents had even more difficulty in the early 1960s.

Zwerg is a native of Appleton, Wisconsin. When I talk to him about his experiences, he easily shares even his most painful memories. Warm and open, Zwerg says he never turns down an opportunity to talk about his civil rights experiences. He views it as his duty.

His parents raised him in the church, where he sang in the choir. He eventually became an Eagle Scout. He says he had wonderful parents who gave him a lot of love and guidance. That changed, though, when he joined the movement.

Zwerg was drawn to the Freedom Rides after he was assigned a black roommate while attending Beloit College in Wisconsin. He grew to admire his roommate and was shocked to see how the young man was treated by whites when they went out in public together. So he volunteered to be an exchange student at Fisk University in Nashville, an all-black college, for one semester. He wanted to know how it felt to be a minority.

Zwerg didn't know it at the time, but he had gone to a city that had become a launching pad for the civil rights movement. While he was there, he was swept up in the group of Nashville college students who were initiating sit-ins and Freedom Rides. He was awed by their commitment and agreed to join them on the bus trip, though he had doubts about whether the nonviolence training he received would prevent him from losing his temper.

Zwerg's parents were unaware of the changes taking place in their son. They were enraged when they opened their local newspaper the day after Zwerg was attacked and saw the now-famous picture of their battered son on the front page.

Zwerg later tried to explain to them that what he did as a Freedom Rider was an outgrowth of what they had taught him, but they remained angry. "These are the two people who instilled my Christian beliefs, my ethics," Zwerg says, "and now they were saying, this time when I lived my faith to the fullest, they didn't accept it."

Zwerg would try to talk to his father about his decision but they could never finish the conversation.

"He'd blow up. He'd say, 'I don't want to talk about it,'" Zwerg tells me. "One time he used the *n*-word. He said, 'Those damn niggers used you.'"

Zwerg's anguish was compounded by his father's weak heart. His father suffered a heart attack after he learned Zwerg was attacked by a mob, and his mother had a nervous breakdown. "I had a tremendous amount of guilt," he says.

Even as the years passed and he was featured in documentaries and history books, Zwerg's parents never gave their approval for what he did. They simply stopped discussing that part of his life.

The closest he got to some sort of reconciliation was a conversation with his mother. She told him that her concern was for his dad. "She said, 'You'll never know the shock. We knew you were doing something, but we learned what happened to you from seeing your picture on the front page of the *Milwaukee Journal*. Until you have a child of your own, you'll never understand.'"

His parents' rejection erased the closeness that Zwerg once felt with them. "I had a lot of anger toward them," he says. "How can they treat me this way? This was the most meaningful period of my life. How could they not understand that?"

Zwerg took out his anger on himself and on others. After the beating, he returned to college but had trouble being close to anyone else. "The two people I loved the most hurt me, so, by God, I wasn't going to love anybody," Zwerg says. "I might meet a girl who I felt was special. One minute I'd tell her that I loved her and the next, I told her I didn't want to see her again."

Zwerg began to drink heavily during his senior year, and at one time he contemplated suicide. Depressed, he remembers putting on his jacket and walking to a pier near campus. He still doesn't remember what happened next. "I remember going out to the pier but I do not remember coming back," he says. "I awoke the next day in my room and when I put on my jacket, a straight-edge razor was in a pocket. I didn't remember putting it there."

Though the aftermath of the beating caused Zwerg much emotional pain, the attack also led to one of the most profound religious experiences of his life. He felt something during the mob attack that he still struggles to describe more than forty years later.

After he stepped off the bus, Zwerg says he and the other Freedom Riders were trying to get quickly to some cars that were supposed to be waiting there for them. But as soon as he stepped off the bus, the crowd grabbed him.

In *Parting the Waters*, Taylor Branch wrote that the mob had swelled to 3,000 people. He described what happened to Zwerg in brutal detail: "One of the men grabbed Zwerg's suitcase and smashed him in the face with it. Others slugged him to the ground, and when he was dazed beyond resistance, one man pinned Zwerg's head between his knees so that the others could take turns hitting him. As they steadily knocked out his teeth, and his face and chest were streaming with blood, a few adults on the perimeter put their children on their shoulders to view the carnage. A small girl asked what the men were doing, and her father replied, 'Well, they're really carrying on.'"

Yet in the midst of that savagery, Zwerg says he had the most beautiful experience in his life. "I bowed my head," he says. "I asked God to give me the strength to remain nonviolent and to forgive the people for what they might do. It was very brief, but in that instant, I felt an overwhelming feeling of a presence with me. I don't know how else to describe it. A peace came over me. I knew that no matter what happened to me, it was going to be OK. Whether I lived or whether I died, I felt this incredible calm."

Zwerg was literally praying when the mob grabbed him. They pulled him over a railing and threw him to the ground. Zwerg said he scampered on all fours to try to make his way back to the other Freedom Riders, but someone kicked him in the spine and he flew forward as a foot came down on his face.

Zwerg blacked out and didn't wake up until he was in the car. The mob had continued to beat him after he was unconscious. Being unconscious saved his life, he believes now. His body was relaxed so it took the punishment better than if he had stiffened up to protect himself. Incredibly, no Freedom Riders were killed during the mob attack.

Even after he was taken to a nearby hospital, Zwerg learned later, he was still not safe. "A nurse said she drugged me the first night I was there because there was a mob coming to within a block of the hospital that was coming to lynch me," he says. "She didn't want me to be aware of anything if they got me."

Zwerg was in such physical shock, he doesn't remember the news crew that did make it to his hospital room. In a scene that was played in the *Eyes on the Prize* documentary, a battered Zwerg told the American public that the Freedom Rides would go on. "We will continue our journey, one way or another. We are prepared to die."

To this day, Zwerg says he doesn't even remember talking to anyone from his hospital bed.

His daughter, though, can't forget the image of her battered father in his hospital bed, still defiant despite his pain. "I cried. I get so proud of him. Every time I meet people, I want to show them the book," she says, referring to *Eyes on the Prize*.

Zwerg's teeth were fractured and several of his vertebrae were cracked, but he recovered. He also took steps to recover emotionally. He was torn between rejoining the Freedom Riders and attending seminary.

Then, as he was being honored by the SCLC for his courage, he talked to Reverend King about his career indecision. "He said, 'Jim, go to seminary. You'll touch a lot more lives through pastoring,'" Zwerg recalls. "Basically, that made up my mind for me."

Mary Brown, the daughter of James Zwerg, today. Her
father's experience remains unfathomable to her.

When he entered seminary, Zwerg decided to go through six
months of therapy to release the anger and guilt he felt toward his parents. He also thought about a woman he had shunned during his angry
college days. "I worked a lot of this through, which made me feel much
better," he says. "When I finished, I knew I wanted to see my lady again.
So, I called her up that night, asked her out, and asked her to marry
me."

That woman, Carolyn, said yes. They live together today in Tucson.

Zwerg entered the ministry after the beating. After pastoring at a
couple of rural churches he became pastor of a large United Church of

Christ (UCC) congregation in Tucson. He became a national leader in the UCC, joining national boards and committees. But he left the ministry in 1975, dejected by the politics of his job.

He bounced around in other jobs. At various times he was a chamber of commerce lobbyist, an IBM manager, and a business manager at a hospice. He worked for a ministry that placed people into low-cost housing. He retired in 1999.

He never found the bond he experienced with the other Freedom Riders anywhere else in his life. "Each of us was stronger because of those we were with," he says. "If I was being beaten, I knew I wasn't alone. I could endure more because I knew everybody there was giving me their strength. Even as someone else was being beaten, I would give them my strength."

Though he became a pastor, Zwerg says his most profound exposure to faith came as a Freedom Rider. "I never felt so alive theologically," he says. "My prayer life was never so meaningful. My whole awareness of the power of love—when I heard King say in his last utterance, 'I've been to the mountaintop and I've seen the Promised Land'— I know those of us who were in the movement can say we were there, too."

But coming down from the mountaintop, after the movement, was deflating, Zwerg says. He couldn't find that bond again. "It's a tremendous downer. You look for it everywhere. I've never experienced it since. The closest thing I've experienced to it is the love of my wife."

Many of his colleagues had the same struggles. As he reunited with his movement friends during civil rights commemorative events, a pattern emerged. Some couldn't keep jobs because they couldn't handle authority. One stepped in front of a bus and killed himself. Another drank himself to death. Many experienced some type of post-traumatic stress syndrome.

Zwerg says he still gets choked up about that morning at the Alabama bus station. When I ask him what emotions he experiences today when he sees that photo of himself at the bus station, Zwerg emits a big sigh and becomes quiet.

Then he tells a story.

He says he recently attended a civil rights reunion at the Birmingham Civil Rights Institute and Museum in Alabama. During a ceremony, Zwerg was walking with a crowd of Freedom Rider colleagues when he saw the famous pictures of his battered face on a video and displayed as a photo on the museum wall.

"I looked at it, and what it brings back to me more than anything else is that I got so much notoriety because I was white," he says. "I looked at that picture and I thought of all the people that never get their names in a book, never get interviewed but literally had given their lives—who the hell am I to have my picture up there?"

He was suddenly flooded with guilt. He started bawling right there during the ceremony as startled people looked on. Then another Freedom Rider veteran, a strapping black man named Jim Davis, walked over to Zwerg.

Zwerg's voice trembles with emotion as he recalls what Davis said. "He said, 'Jim, you don't realize that it was your words from that hospital bed that were the call to arms for the rest of us.'"

And then, as Davis wrapped his big arms around Zwerg in front of the startled crowd, the two men cried together.

Maisha Moses
Daughter of Bob Moses

THE VOICE ON THE PHONE IS INSTANTLY RECOGNIZABLE, a Boston-accented monotone that barely rises above a whisper. The speaking style is also distinctive: ambling sentences that suddenly trail off into periods of silence that are so long I have to say hello to make sure the speaker is still there.

No civil rights leader sounds like Bob Moses, a SNCC leader who seemed to break all the rules for becoming a movement legend. The Harvard-trained mathematician couldn't fire up a crowd, hated personal attention, and rarely spoke above a mumble. Yet no SNCC leader inspired the veneration Moses did by working virtually alone in rural Mississippi during the early 1960s trying to register black voters—a kind of suicide mission in that era.

The voice on the telephone line, however, doesn't belong to Bob Moses. It belongs to his eldest daughter, Maisha, thirty-two, who sounds uncannily like her father. She is talking to me about what movement veterans call the Bob Moses mystique—the captivating effect her father has on people. "I understand why they feel like that," Maisha says. "I see it. I experience it sometimes in Mississippi. I go to places and people say, 'Oh, this is Bob Moses's daughter,' and it's such a big thing."

Moses's mystique is rooted in his resilience. Few civil rights leaders endured such a prolonged exposure to cruelty. He was beaten and shot at; several of the people he persuaded to work alongside him in Mississippi were murdered. He had no federal marshals or sympathetic politicians to protect him. Yet he pressed on, never seeming to lose his Zen-like calm.

But in 1966 the tension caught up with Bob Moses. He suffered what some describe as an emotional breakdown. He left the South and abandoned his civil rights colleagues, changed his name, and fled to

Courtesy of the Library of Congress

Bob Moses at a 1964 press conference. The murders of three civil rights workers that Mississippi Freedom Summer would contribute to the burden of guilt Moses felt over the loss of lives.

Tanzania in 1969. There he started a family. He didn't return to the United States until 1976.

Though I had read plenty about Bob Moses in Mississippi, I didn't know much about those seven years he spent in Tanzania. But after talking with his daughter I began to see that what he accomplished in Tanzania was just as impressive as what he had accomplished in Mississippi.

Many movement veterans have never been able to find another cause in the second half of life. And many have not been able to build close relationships with their children. They lead lives that are adrift, rarely connecting with anyone or anything.

But Bob Moses broke that pattern. He left his mystique behind and discovered a new cause in his middle years, and an unlikely partner—his daughter, Maisha.

Their cause is the Algebra Project. It is a program Bob Moses created in 1982, which now reaches 10,000 students in ten states.

The premise is straightforward: a student's economic success hinges on algebraic competence because it's a requirement for a college-prep curriculum. No algebra, no college, no success.

At first, I couldn't see the connection between the Mississippi Freedom Summer and algebra. But Moses says mathematical literacy functions like the voting poll tax functioned during segregation: both are devices to lock blacks out of mainstream America. "Kids are being told that algebra is not for them just like sharecroppers were told that voting was not for them," Moses says.

The project was inspired by Maisha. When she was in eighth grade, her father was so frustrated that the school didn't offer algebra he asked his daughter's teacher if he could teach algebra to his daughter at the school. (He had taught math at a New York City prep school from 1958 to 1961).

The teacher not only said yes, but asked Moses if he could teach three of Maisha's classmates as well. The Algebra Project was born.

Today, Maisha works alongside her father at Lanier High School in Jackson, Mississippi. It is an inner-city school with a predominately black student body. Maisha is a Harvard University graduate and, like her father, an avid swimmer who meditates and practices yoga.

Maisha never saw a "For Whites Only" sign, but she did experience a more subtle form of segregation called tracking, the steering of black students to classes that weren't designed to prepare students for college. When she was assigned regular-level classes in junior high school, Maisha says her mother, Janet (also a former SNCC member), made her return to school and demand honors courses. Maisha was then assigned college preparatory classes in math and science.

Maisha says some of her friends told her she was taking college preparatory courses because she was smart, but it wasn't that simple. "I was always either the only one or maybe one of two blacks in the classes. It was real clear that it had nothing to do with how smart I was but just that my parents had made sure the system worked for me."

Maisha's father continued to expand the project. By the time she entered Harvard, Maisha spent her spare time tutoring elementary school students. When she graduated she decided to devote herself full-time to the project because she thought of how close she had come to being excluded from college at an early age.

She also joined because of the project's unique approach. "It's the type of work when you have small changes over a long period of time," she says. "The problems are so deep and so widespread that it's like you can grow into it."

The project's teaching method is to demystify algebra by using real-world lessons. Teachers mix lemonade from concentrate to teach ratios and proportions. Students ride trains to learn about integers. They learn to represent mathematical concepts by drawing or even rapping about them. "It's part of their culture," Maisha says. "They teach each other video games, clapping games on the [basketball] court; it's part of youth culture to teach others the things they like to do and they're interested in."

Maisha says working alongside her father feels like a natural progression. While she was growing up, her parents told her about their work in Mississippi. They taught her freedom songs. "Growing up like that sort of makes you feel like you have a responsibility to help out and try to do something to make things better. It was never, 'You have to do this.' Nobody even said you have a responsibility to this. It was just people telling their stories about what they did. That's what you're around. That's what you soak up."

She says the project is a continuation of the movement. "The movement in the early 1960s was the culmination of all this energy that had been building for years that sort of came to a head and erupted. But

it was relatively short-lived. The work we're doing now is in that building phase of gathering energy that may culminate in a similar type of
movement. This is more of a gathering energy."

Bob Moses says it's "deeply gratifying" to work alongside his daughter. Three of his remaining children have also worked within the Algebra Project.

I meet Bob Moses at the Birmingham Civil Rights Institute; he has
taken a busload of Algebra Project students to the civil rights museum
there. I immediately understand why people gravitate to him. Part of it
is his humility. When his class sits down to listen to speakers, Moses
doesn't sit in the front row. He sits in the middle with the students. And
when a speaker asks Moses to come up and talk about his civil rights
activism, he walks instead to the front of the room and asks his students to talk about their experiences in the Algebra Project.

Then there is his extraordinary personal presence. He exudes tran-
quility—eyes intently focusing on the person talking to him, never getting flustered. I now see why frightened people would be drawn to his
calmness in a war zone like Mississippi in 1964. Now sixty-nine, and a
vegetarian, Moses still walks with the bounce of a young man. He
swims 2,000 yards a day.

When I ask him about his mystique, he says he once grew tired of
hearing about it, but it doesn't bother him anymore. "For a long time,
I didn't read anything about myself," he says. "I've gotten to the point
where I can read things and not let them affect me."

He explains that there were no initial plans to have his daughter
join him. But when he was in SNCC, he occasionally talked to his colleagues about how they could remain activists as they grew older and
had families.

"In SNCC, we were in our early twenties," he says. "We didn't really
have personal family responsibilities or personal job responsibilities

except movement work. If we're going to have families and have different kinds of jobs other than just movement work, one question came: can SNCC evolve in a way to accommodate those demands?"

Bob Moses struggled with the demands of being a leader in SNCC as well. His personality made him stand out from the beginning. It wasn't just that he was brave; almost all the SNCC members were courageous. He was also smart. He was a Harvard graduate who quoted Camus and traveled to Japan for a year to study Zen Buddhism—he was one of the few civil rights leaders who could match Dr. King's spiritual and intellectual depths.

On the other hand, his leadership style was so different from King's, says Taylor Branch. "He was the anti-King. He turned every rule of oratory upside down. He practically whispered when he talked. But he was able to project sincerity and a real mental wrestling with tough problems in an unflinching way."

Courtesy of the Atlanta Constitution

Maisha Moses, hugging her father, Bob Moses, at Lanier High School in Jackson, Mississippi, where she helps him run the Algebra Project.

Moses was unlike King in another significant way, Branch says. Bob Moses had trouble accepting the notion that people were going to die. "He was obsessed with the burden of leadership and the trail of sacrifice behind him, that when people did what he told [them to do], some lost their lives. I think that ate at him a lot. I think that was part of his breakdown. He wasn't like Martin Luther King, who was a tough-minded general. Martin Luther King knew that there were going to be people who died."

Bob Moses helped create Mississippi Freedom Summer, the voting registration project that drew white Northern students to the state to work alongside black civil rights workers in 1964. But when three of those workers were murdered that summer, Branch says Moses was haunted by constant self-examination. Was he complicit in their deaths? Was he complicit in the earlier deaths of people like Herbert Lee, a black activist killed while trying to register black voters in Mississippi?

In 1966 Moses convened a final meeting with SNCC members and, after passing around a block of cheese and a jug of wine, he told them, "I want you to eat and drink." The incident, recorded in Branch's *Pillar of Fire*, was widely interpreted as a sign that the civil rights leader had reached his emotional end.

Afterward he drifted into antiwar activism. When he was drafted at thirty-one in 1967, he thought the government was targeting him. He fled to Canada and later moved to Tanzania in 1969 with his wife, Janet.

Moses says he fled the country because he was thinking of having a family. "The real choice, in hindsight, was leaving and doing family versus staying and doing more movement," he says. "It would have been hard to stay and do family."

He says he once struggled with the notion that he was "using" lives in Mississippi. When I ask him about being plagued by feelings of guilt, he quickly answers. "I think more that the responsibility was making sure that I honor their demise with my life. When Herbert Lee was murdered in 1961, what we were able to say and eventually do was offer our commitment to continuing this struggle. So that kind of eases the responsibility, the feeling that maybe this is all kind of using some-body."

Maisha says the time in Tanzania helped her father recover from the pressures of the movement. They lived in a two-bedroom home in a remote area, with mountains in the background and open land all around. When she stepped outside, she couldn't even see any other houses. "It just seemed calmer, it seemed slower paced," she says. "That kind of space and openness, living without pressure, was healing. The focus was just on raising us."

In Tanzania, Moses taught math, but he was also a stay-at-home dad, cooking the majority of the meals and changing diapers while his wife attended medical school.

It was there that Maisha first learned to take education seriously. African schools were strict. Her mother, Janet Moses, can still see Maisha trotting off to first grade with a hoe over her shoulder so she could work in the school garden with other students.

Janet says school in Tanzania was a serious affair. Many of the schools were throwbacks to one-room schoolhouses with students squeezed together on long benches. Many of her daughter's classmates had to run several miles to get there each day. "I think you develop a sense of what is really important—there's no dancing around the edges of learning, or teaching, for that matter. Maisha has had a pattern in her life of having to make do with grace and having to surrender ego for a greater good, of taking on challenges and thriving in rigorous situations."

Bob Moses says he was able to get away from his mystique in Tanzania. They had few visitors. Hardly anyone came to talk about the movement or to ask for his time. "You were free of all of that to really concentrate on raising the kids," he says. "I've always felt that it was a blessing. Tanzania turned out to be a good choice to recuperate and also to pay attention to family and to get ready, as it turns out, to reenter."

Moses returned to Cambridge, Massachusetts, in 1976 after incoming President Jimmy Carter offered draft amnesty. His eldest daughter says she experienced culture shock. She didn't speak English; she wasn't accustomed to the fast pace of American life or the way that young children talked to their elders. The family also had to adjust to living in a country where black people were a minority. Janet Moses says she was riding the bus one day when her oldest son, Omo, asked, "Where did all the black people go?"

Within two weeks of arriving in the United States, Maisha and her brother stopped speaking to each other in Swahili. She remembers putting a pillowcase on her head at home to pretend that she had long, flowing hair. "I don't know where or how I got that message," she says. "I'm sure it had to do with going to school with white people."

She had to make another adjustment when she grew older and started hearing about her father's mystique. She says she could identify with some of the perceptions about her father. "He's very serious and focused," she says. "He doesn't do a lot of chit-chat. Sometimes it's hard because sometimes you want to joke around."

Maisha used to wonder why her father was so serious, but she now thinks it has to do with his time in Mississippi. She recalls hearing her father talk with Dave Dennis, another SNCC member, about the brutality they experienced trying to register black voters in Mississippi. "They said it was like you live a lifetime in four years," she says. "It's so concentrated. It's so intense. And people paid heavy prices for that."

When I ask her if the mystique ever intimidated her, she laughs. "Not a whole lot. He's always had a high standard."

Maisha is more impressed by her father as a parent than as an activist. She never felt like she took a backseat to her father's position. "I just have so much love and respect for him as a person, not just for the work he's done," she says. "He's always been very present throughout all of our lives. Being a father to us was always the most important thing to him."

2

The Next Generation

WHERE DO WE GO FROM HERE? That was the title of the last book written by Martin Luther King Jr. It's also the question children of civil rights activists face when searching for their own role.

The "For Whites Only" signs are relegated to museums. Civil rights groups such as the NAACP and the Southern Christian Leadership Conference (SCLC) don't command the national stage anymore. Saying you want to be a civil rights activist doesn't elicit the same respect it once did.

So you become something else. Those profiled in this chapter are the sons and daughters of some of the biggest names in the civil rights movement. They don't call themselves civil rights activists, but they all insist that in their own way they are carrying on their families' tradition. The son of Ralph David Abernathy Sr. explains why his ascent to political prominence ended in a jail cell. The son of Julian Bond recalls how his sense of mission was formed by a devastating family scandal. The eldest son of former Student Nonviolent Coordinating Committee (SNCC) leader James Forman has created a school for those the civil rights movement left behind. The daughter of Lawrence Guyot, an SNCC field secretary, talks about being biracial, having "good hair," and encountering racial stereotypes in the most unexpected places. And the only son of Andrew Young, a member of Martin Luther King's inner circle, explains how he's fighting for a new type of integration.

Ralph David Abernathy III
Son of Ralph David Abernathy Sr.

RALPH DAVID ABERNATHY III GLIDES into the downtown Atlanta restaurant thirty minutes late but with the unhurried ease of a man who operates on his own time.

He has picked the City Grill, a posh restaurant where the city's prominent politicians and business leaders gather, as the place to meet me. As the jaunty melody from "Take Five" drifts from the speakers, Ralph settles in to explain the bizarre turns his life has recently taken.

Not long ago, he was an up-and-coming Georgia state senator. He had name recognition. He was the forty-five-year-old son of Ralph David Abernathy Sr., Martin Luther King Jr.'s best friend. And he had a position of political power to add to his family's legacy.

Ralph dutifully talks about a series of ugly public incidents that derailed his career, but he prefers to concentrate on his future. He says he's a new man. God has called him to be a pastor just like his father. His days of grabbing headlines are over. "I'm being very low profile," he says, sipping hot tea. "Where the Lord leads me, that's where I'm going to follow."

Two days later, I see a stunned-looking Ralph being led away in handcuffs. He is on the evening news, wearing an orange jailhouse jumpsuit while being arraigned in an Atlanta courthouse. He has just been arrested for bilking two women out of $35,000.

No other child of a civil rights leader has followed a path as exasperating as that of Ralph Abernathy. Bad fortune sticks to him like lint to an old sweater. During my talk with him, he blames all his problems on outside forces that have conspired to bring him down. "If my name had been anything else other than Ralph David Abernathy, I certainly wouldn't have gone to prison for $5,700," he says. "I mean, they blew up everything."

Ralph's bitterness isn't just connected to his personal misfortune. Some of it also comes from his belief that his father and family have never gotten the credit they deserved, especially from King's family.

Ralph's anger doesn't square with the public perception of the relationship between the two families. His father's close friendship with King is well documented. The night before he was assassinated in Memphis, King told an audience that Ralph David Abernathy Sr. was "my best friend in the whole world." The two men seemed inseparable. Abernathy Sr. was with King in 1955 when his public career started with the Montgomery Bus Boycott. He accompanied King through virtually all his major campaigns. And in 1968 he cradled a dying King in his arms after the shooting on the balcony of a Memphis motel.

Abernathy Sr. went on to lead the SCLC in King's place before resigning in 1977. He died in 1990 from heart failure. Two years before his death, though, Abernathy Sr. saw his eldest son get elected to the

Courtesy of Birmingham Public Library

Ralph David Abernathy Sr., center, marches with Martin Luther King Jr. and Fred Shuttlesworth in Birmingham in 1963.

Georgia House at the age of twenty-eight. He never lived to see the bizarre turns his son's political career would take.

Ralph's early political career unfolded without incident. Four years later, in 1992, he was elected to the Georgia Senate.

But then Ralph began making the news.

In January 1994 he was cited and fined for leading police on a high-speed chase. He told the media that he was headed to an elementary school to give an inspirational speech to students. Ralph explained to an *Atlanta Constitution* reporter afterward why he didn't slow down for officers. "The breaking of the speed limit was justified in achieving the goal that I had, which was to give a speech before school let out. Those people gave me a standing ovation."

Six months later, a woman complained that Ralph barged in on her and refused to leave while she was in an unmarked restroom stall in the Georgia state capitol building.

There were other embarrassing public incidents. In 1997 customs officials at Atlanta's Hartsfield International Airport searched Ralph's luggage and found marijuana hidden in his underwear. The next year he was disqualified from running for the state senate seat he was expected to reclaim; the $400 check he used to pay his qualifying fee bounced. And in December 1999 a Fulton County Superior Court jury found him guilty of theft involving $5,700 in state funds and violation of his oath of office. He was sentenced to four years in prison. He served sixteen months.

In 2002, when Ralph had been out of prison for a year and a half, he was sent back to jail. A Georgia parole board found Ralph guilty of taking $35,000 from two women after promising to win the release of their loved ones from prison. A Georgia law prohibits anyone other than a lawyer from receiving fees to speak on behalf of inmates before the parole board.

Reverend Hosea Williams, one of King's top lieutenants, in one of his last interviews before his death in 2000, publicly scolded Ralph: "The life that little Ralph is living, unfortunately, does diminish his father's legacy. To me, it's the greatest hurt."

But Ralph has an explanation for every incident. In person, he bears an uncanny likeness to his father: the same fleshy, stubble face, stocky build, even the same slow, Southern Baptist cadences to his speech. "They blew up everything," he says of the run-ins he has had with the law.

"Didn't you really have marijuana when they stopped you at the airport?" I ask him.

"The marijuana in the underwear was one marijuana cigarette," he says.

"How about the high-speed chase that ended at an elementary school?"

"I never got a ticket. I never was arrested."

"The woman in the bathroom?"

"That was purely me walking into the wrong bathroom and saying, 'Oh my God, I'm sorry,' turning around and walking out, and her cussing at me."

"The conviction and four-year prison term for stealing $5,700 in state money?"

Ralph lowers his head and remains silent before answering. "It was tough," he says. "I didn't sit up and whine. You didn't see me kicking and hollering. Oh yeah, they dogged me out. They had me picking collard greens and strawberries out in the field. I was working on the chain gang."

The only time Ralph's defiance seems to waver comes when I read complaints about his behavior from Hosea Williams and other King confidants. He lowers his head in resignation and sighs as he hears me repeat comments about how he has diminished his father's legacy.

"If that's their feeling, that's fine," he says. "They deserve to have their own opinions. But I disagree with them. I cannot diminish the legacy of my father. All I can do is diminish my own legacy. There's nothing I can do or say that can take away my father's contributions because my father's contributions are etched in American history."

He says it was more difficult explaining to his wife and kids about why he had to go to jail. When I ask him what he told his children, he

Ralph Abernathy III, when he was a Georgia state senator In 1998, is flanked by civil rights activists Reverend Hosea Williams, right, and Georgia State Representative Tyrone Brooks, left, on the steps of the Georgia Capitol as he talks about the check he bounced for the Democratic Party filing fee. He told members of the media that the funds were in his wife's account at the time the check was written.

evokes his father's memory. "I told them, the way Granddaddy went to prison for justice, Daddy went to prison for injustice."

For Ralph, all of his bad fortune can be tied to his potential for greatness. "I think the people had seen my style of politics and listened to me speak, the power structure had observed me," he says. "I think they realized that I had probably gotten it."

When I ask what he possessed that would alarm the power structure, Ralph stops stirring his tea, smiles, and seems to contemplate whether I can handle what he's about to reveal to me. Then he finally says, "The calling to lead the people."

When he sees the quizzical look on my face, he leans forward in his chair to explain his point. "Much like my father and Martin, somebody got it. Where did it go? It doesn't just disappear. It's passed on to the next generation."

Ralph maintains that neither of King's two sons, Martin Luther III nor Dexter, has the leadership ability he possesses. "If you watched me in the Senate and observed my style, my charisma, the way all of my colleagues loved me in the state capitol. . . . I was an up-and-coming, very influential legislator. I got a highway named after my father. Come on."

Ralph's belief that outside forces have conspired to deny his greatness isn't confined to him. It runs in the family. His father felt the same way, according to Andrew Young, a member of King's inner circle. "Ralph's daddy was screwed up," he told me. "He was in over his head. Martin Luther King needed Ralph Abernathy but Ralph Abernathy never quite understood spiritually what Martin Luther King was all about. That's reflected in only one child. The two girls and Kwame [Ralph's two sisters and younger brother] are solid as a rock."

Tension between Ralph's family and movement veterans is nothing new. Much of it spilled out into the open in 1989 when Abernathy Sr. published his autobiography, *And the Walls Came Tumbling Down*, in which he said King was sexually intimate with three women the night before he was assassinated. He also stated that King frequently used foul language.

Young said Abernathy Sr. projected his own personal struggles onto King. "Ralph's daddy had a trifling streak in him, an irresponsible streak, a greedy streak about food, about money, about power, and about sex. He passed it off in his book. He tried to attribute it all to Martin. It was ridiculous."

In Young's book, *An Easy Burden*, he said Abernathy Sr. had sacrificed his own preaching career to help promote King when he first met him in the days before the Montgomery Bus Boycott. Over time King began to rely on Abernathy Sr. partly because the latter was so willing to go to jail with him. Young said King was terrified of being left alone in jail.

But Abernathy Sr. was also envious of King's growing prominence. He felt that he should have received the Nobel Peace Prize along with King. He also thought King should make amends for the oversight by giving him half of the prize money, Young said. "Ralph loved Martin, but as often happens with brothers, he was also jealous of him," Young wrote.

The bitterness that Abernathy Sr. felt seems to have been absorbed by some of his family members. When King was alive, the Abernathy children called him Uncle Martin and his wife Aunt Coretta. The King children called Abernathy Sr. Uncle Ralph. After Abernathy Sr.'s death, underlying tensions between the family members came to light.

After her husband's funeral in 1990, Juanita Abernathy publicly complained that the local newspaper published a front-page photo of Mrs. King in attendance, but failed to print a front-page photo of *her*. During another interview with the *Atlanta Constitution*, Mrs. Abernathy bristled when Mrs. King's name was brought up. "I thought this was supposed to be about me," she told the reporter.

Ralph tells me he believes the King family deliberately prevented his father from receiving more recognition. "Aunt Coretta had her own self-ish reasons for lifting him up. My father loved Martin—that was his boy. He didn't fight it because he was authentic. He didn't have a need for anybody to push him up because he wanted to see Martin pushed up. He recognized that Martin was a leader."

Ralph says he knows why the King family doesn't want to give credit to his father. "The King family's whole point is to elevate Martin for prosperity and monetary reasons. They're making millions of dollars off of Martin. They don't want to share that limelight."

But he insists that his father was just as important to the movement as King. "Every time Martin Luther King spoke, my father spoke," he says. "One spoke about the philosophy. The other spoke about the strategy. They were a team. Every time Martin would go to jail, my father went to jail. There had to be a leader, but my father was a coleader. There was a partnership. My father wasn't Martin Luther King's lieutenant. He wasn't like Jesse, Andy, and Hosea."

Despite his negative feelings about the King family, Ralph says he's still friends with all of them. He attended elementary school with Dexter, King's youngest son, and even shared an apartment with him once. But he's never talked with any King family members about his belief that they refused to give credit to his father. "We do not talk about this. I think they have their own spin on it, and it's been given to them by their own mother. They justify it by however they justify it. We just leave it alone and go on."

He also says that "white America" had a part in denying his father credit: they went along with the King family's decision to hide the contributions of his father because they were afraid. "Can you imagine how America would have benefited to see Martin and Ralph together, like Bobby Kennedy and John Kennedy? Can you imagine what that would have done to young black kids? There'd be young black kids walking around here—one would say, 'I can't be Martin Luther King, but maybe together we could be King and Abernathy.' "

What Ralph imagines for his future now is a place in the pulpit. His goal is to pastor his own church. "I was called to the ministry in 1999," he says. "Several members of my church, people who have known me all my life, say I was called to the ministry a long time ago, including my mother. But I just didn't accept it. I think to a great degree they are right."

Ralph says there's no chance he will enter politics again. It can't compare with the feeling he gets when he preaches. "There are chills all over my body whenever I step into a pulpit and preach. I compromised my call and went into politics as a way to say, 'Look, Lord, I don't want to preach, but I will serve.' "

He said Young called him on his second day in prison and told him to read the Bible. "That's why I'm not bitter; I'm better. And when you're better, you can't be bitter. Prison fine-tuned me. Spiritually, I became closer to God. I had time to study."

He also used the time to fine-tune himself physically. Young told him to take his mattress off of his bed and put it on the floor of his jail cell to run in place. It's the same exercise regimen that Nelson Mandela used when he was a political prisoner. "I ran every day I was in prison," he says. "I still do it today. I run in place. I run on the carpet in my home. I like running in place. I don't have to get up and go. I don't have to dress. It's better than running on a track."

It's getting dark, and Ralph has to leave. As we walk outside, Ralph asks me not to make him look bad—so many people are out to destroy his family's name. But he says his family's enemies won't win in the end. "You can't kill us," he says. "You can't destroy us. You can't break us. This has just made us stronger. You cannot break a family that has been one of the leading families that helped changed the course of this country."

Two days later, Ralph is back in jail, contemplating conspiracies from his cell, reading his Bible—still running in place.

Michael Julian Bond
Son of Julian Bond

FIRST CAME THE HUMILIATING HEADLINES, the embarrassing public disclosures, the reporters who trailed his family like paparazzi. Then there were the whispers he heard in public. Some people even came right up to him and asked if the stories about his father were really true. "I think they wanted to see me break down, cry, wail, and moan," says Michael Bond. "I just wasn't going to give them that satisfaction."

Michael has always been proud to be the son of civil rights hero Julian Bond. His father first burst into prominence as a leader in Student Nonviolent Coordinating Committee (SNCC) and as a twenty-five-year-old Georgia senator who was barred from taking his seat because he opposed the Vietnam War. Media-polished, urbane, and handsome, Julian Bond was literally the voice of the movement. His commanding voice provided the narration for the epic civil rights documentary *Eyes on the Prize*.

But over a two-year period, Michael watched his father's life turn into a soap opera: a shocking political loss, a nasty feud that ended his friendship with another civil rights leader, and public speculation that Julian Bond was a cocaine user.

A low point came when Michael's mother, Alice, got involved in a tussling, cursing fight with his father's alleged mistress in public. She and Julian divorced after that incident.

Michael's father reacted to the turn of events by not reacting. Julian refused to talk about it publicly and eventually moved out of Atlanta after the scandal to find a new career and new wife. "I'm not much for public self-analysis," he told a reporter at the time of the scandal. "My agonies are my agonies. Aren't your agonies your agonies?"

But Julian Bond's agony became his son's agony. The events that ended his father's political career dug into Michael, and the wounds still linger. "That sobered me on life a lot," Michael says of the trauma of his father's political flameout. "My rose-colored glasses were cracked."

Today, Michael, thirty-six, is the deputy director of the Atlanta branch of the NAACP. He is divorced and the father of three children, ages twelve, fourteen, and fifteen.

I meet him in Atlanta's empty city council chambers. The setting is familiar to him: he was an important Atlanta city council member until 2002, when he lost a run-off election for council president. The vote, which came after Michael led in the initial polls, surprised many in Atlanta.

After the vote, the *Atlanta Constitution* wrote a story about Michael's loss. The newspaper sent a photographer to capture Michael moving out of his city council office. But he refused to have his picture taken, saying it sent the wrong message. He plans to return to politics one day. Eventually, he wants to be the mayor of Atlanta. "This is so much fun for me, being here at City Hall," he says, gesturing around the carpeted chambers. "From these seats, you can do whatever you want."

As he talks about his days in Atlanta's city council, Michael seems to revel in the everyday details of being a politician: building a road that a community desperately needed, putting up traffic lights, creating job-training bills. Initially wary when he met me (I worked for the same Atlanta newspaper that Michael believes hounded his father), Michael relaxes and brightens up as he talks about the fun he has had in his career.

Jason Johnson, a childhood friend of Michael's who attended More-house College with him, recalls one time when Michael tracked him down overseas to tell him that he had improved a notoriously blighted road in his council district. "I was in Germany when he called and said, 'Hey Jason, I just got Simpson Road paved.' To Mike, that was just as important as his biggest accomplishment because it benefited the community."

Yet Michael concedes that being a politician isn't as prestigious and well paying as other careers now open to blacks. "I don't need a lot of

Courtesy of the Library of Congress

A boyish-looking Julian Bond waits to take center stage at the beginning of his political career on January 26, 1966.

money," he says. "I've never been motivated by money. I like being here. I like doing the things you can do to help people. It's a greater reward to see the appreciation on people's faces. It stays longer."

Michael has long been accustomed to being around politicians. He was born the same year his father won his first political seat. One of his first memories is of seeing his father at the tumultuous 1968 Democratic Convention in Chicago, where he was nominated for the vice presidency by a group of Democrats looking for a symbol of revolt. Bond asked that the nomination be withdrawn because, at 28, he was too young to serve.

"I remember seeing my father on television," Michael recalls. "I was trying to touch him through the television screen." As a kid, Michael saw his father appear on television so often that he thought that was his actual job. The only time Michael was really impressed with his father's television appearances came when Julian hosted *Saturday Night Live* in 1977.

Michael was made aware early in life that he belonged to a family of achievers. His grandfather was Horace Mann Bond, former president of Lincoln University in Pennsylvania and a dean of Atlanta University's School of Education. In Horace Bond's home, people like Albert Einstein, W. E. B. Du Bois, and sociologist E. Franklin Frazier were visitors.

Independent thinking was also encouraged by his father, even when it came to mundane matters. "My father always challenged me intellectually. Whenever I would ask to go to Six Flags [an Atlanta amusement park] or Burger King or something, he would challenge me on it. 'Why do you want to do that? What is it going to gain you?' I had to come up with the reasons why."

His father's home also featured its share of big names. Virtually all the civil rights leaders—Andrew Young, John Lewis, and Jesse Jackson—called or visited constantly. "It was like being in an extended family," he says.

Watching this extended family gain political power was thrilling. After the civil rights movement ebbed during the late 1960s, many of its leaders settled in Atlanta. Maynard Jackson became the city's first black mayor when Michael was in elementary school. Andrew Young followed him.

Once Michael's father took him to visit Young just after Young had become mayor. "We went over to see Andy and he had his shoes off on the desk, relaxed, and he had all these people wanting to see him, but he let us in first," Michael says. "They [Michael's father and Young] were talking about me applying for a summer job and Andy says, 'What kind of job do you want, Michael?' I said, 'I want your job. I want to do what you're doing.' "

Michael saw, though, that the life of a public official left little room for private time. When he and his family went out to a restaurant, his father was often besieged by people asking for his autograph—or for something more. "All kind of folks came up to him with problems, whether they were broke, discriminated against, or homeless," Michael says. "He never let anything go without looking into it, even if he couldn't fix it."

Michael treasured the time he could spend with his father. When Julian came home late at night, Michael stayed up watching Johnny Carson with him. When his father would go to the newsstand to read, he'd trail along. He grabbed every moment he could with his father. "I used to joke with my friends that I had to go make an appointment and see him, but I did," Michael says. "I just kind of understood that this guy is busy and I like what he's doing, I believe in what he's doing. I'm going to try to fit in where I can because I know he has a lot on his plate."

When his father was busy traveling, Michael yearned for his presence. When he was playing soccer, he'd look out in vain to see if his father had showed up. If he went to a PTA meeting, he saw his friends with their fathers, and he wished his was with him. "I used to even miss his scent," Michael says. "He had a closet downstairs in our house. All of his clothes were down there. If you opened the door, you could smell him, but he wasn't there."

Michael decided early on that he wouldn't complain about his father's absences or let his friends see him sad. He was a Bond, and like his father, he wanted to keep his agony private. "There are so many jealous and spiteful people in the world. You don't want to give them the benefit of letting them see you looking sad. I'd just tough it out and act like it didn't bother me."

As he grew older, Michael felt the weight of his last name in other ways, too. When he heard or read about the children of other civil rights leaders who got into trouble, he thought about the consequences to his family's name if he did the same. "I always wanted to learn from other people's mistakes," he says. "When I would hear my parents talk about kids of notable parents and how screwed up the kids were, I was like, oh no, I don't want to be the one to be talked about."

Yet Michael decided to enter politics, a field in which scrutiny was unrelenting. He ran for a seat in the Georgia House but lost by a narrow margin. Then he won a seat in Atlanta's city council. His victory fulfilled a childhood ambition. But his father wasn't happy. "He actually tried to talk me out of it many times," Michael says. "He would say, 'Politics is a dirty business. People are cutthroat.' All I could see was the good you could achieve by being there."

Julian Bond, who currently serves as the board chairman of the NAACP, says he felt that his son was too young to enter politics. "It's a hard life, an unforgiving life," he says. "It's an insecure life. You don't want your children to have any of that. It's one of the few professions in which your job is rated by thousands of people that don't even know you. You're on top today and you're on your behind tomorrow."

Julian Bond speaks from experience. In 1986, he ran for Atlanta's fifth congressional seat. His opponent was John Lewis—another civil rights hero, Michael's godfather, and Julian's best friend. Their friendship had been forged in the SNCC in the early 1960s. "Our families were so close," Michael says. "They had been inseparable for years. As kids, we'd love going over to their house. We loved John and [his wife] almost like we loved our parents."

But the election fight soon turned bitter. During the campaign, Lewis hinted that Bond took cocaine and other drugs, and challenged him to take a public drug test to prove him wrong.

The race even brought to the surface ugly remnants of the plantation system. Some people saw Bond, the fair-skinned, highly educated member of one of black America's elite families, as a "house Negro." They saw Lewis, a dark-skinned son of a poor Southern family, as a "field negro." These references date back to the days of slavery when darker-skinned slaves were often relegated to field work while lighter-skinned slaves were used in the master's house.

Julian Bond lost the election, a fact he blamed on Lewis's willingness to play dirty.

The friendship between the two men ended. During one debate, Bond turned to Lewis and said, "We've been friends for twenty-five years. We went to Africa together. We were in Selma together . . . but never in those twenty-five years did I ever hear any of the things you are saying about me now. Why did I have to wait twenty-five years to find out what you really thought of me, to find out that you really don't think I amount to much?"

Michael says Lewis told lies about his father. For example, in Lewis's autobiography, *Walking with the Wind*, Lewis says Julian Bond's legs trembled when he first told him he was going to run against him. "I was there," Michael says, shaking his head in disgust. "My father's leg was not trembling. He was going to whip John very convincingly. That would have happened if not for John's negative campaigning."

Michael was filled with disbelief when Lewis hinted that his father used drugs. "There was a lot about John Lewis my father could have unloaded that would have ended his public career, period, in all senses of the word," Michael says. "But my father chose not to campaign negatively."

Michael's relationship with Lewis is now "very cordial." But they've never talked about the election. No one brings it up. He says Lewis and his father are no longer friends.

The next year, another bomb dropped. His mother, Alice, walked into an Atlanta police station and told officers three things: her husband had used cocaine for four years, his mistress was one of his suppliers, and many other prominent Atlantans used cocaine too.

The news exploded in the media. Julian Bond's alleged mistress was jailed on charges of cocaine trafficking. Even Andrew Young, who was mayor of Atlanta at the time, got caught up in the events. He was summoned by a federal grand jury to explain whether or not a telephone call he made to Alice Bond was designed to hush her up.

The scandal became so big that the *Atlanta Constitution* assigned twenty-seven reporters to cover it—including photographers who trailed Michael's sister to her prom in the hope of catching up with Julian, Michael says. The publicity got so bad that Michael walked into the newspaper's office and confronted reporters about the articles about his family.

The reaction from the public was almost as painful as the event itself. Michael says that when he went out in public, people made comments and asked him questions. He refused to answer. He kept his hurt to himself.

"If I ever wanted to make a name for myself and have my children be proud of me, I couldn't crack," he says. "I'm stubborn. I just didn't want to give these people the satisfaction of destroying my family, which is what they were trying to do."

In the end, Julian Bond was not charged with any drug use. He and his wife divorced. He then left Atlanta and took a position as a

Courtesy of Michael Bond

Michael Bond, left, with his father, Julian, today. They remain close, but family scandal exacted a price from them both.

distinguished scholar in residence at the American University in Washington, D.C. He has since remarried.

Perhaps because of these events Michael gained more incentive to enter politics. He felt his father had been forced to leave Atlanta under a cloud. "I wanted to go into politics to prove these critics and the people who tried to tear my family down wrong," he says. "I first decided to run for office right after my parents' divorce. People said you shouldn't use your father's name because it's negative. That insulted me. I'm very proud of my family, in particular my father, so I kept it."

Jason Johnson confirms that Michael's father's election loss and his parents' divorce wounded Michael. But it also gave him motivation. "He wanted to prove that others were wrong about the family and what they stood for." And the scandal revealed a side of Michael that many people don't know exists—his pugnacious nature. "He was very tenacious," Johnson says. "You kick the beehive and here comes Mike. He's not going to roll over. He's coming out to sting."

That side of Michael apparently remains hidden from his father as well. Today, Julian Bond still refuses to talk about that episode in his life. When I ask him how the scandal affected his relationship with Michael, Bond cuts me off before I finish my question. "Now you're crossing the line," he says. He says he doesn't want to appeal to the "prurient" interest of readers by talking about his family's business.

When I ask him if he thinks his family's name was damaged by the scandal, Bond cuts my question short again. "Now you're crossing the line again," he says. But he goes on to tell me that he doesn't think his family's name was damaged by the scandal. He says he didn't know that part of his son's mission in politics was vindicating the family's honor. "I haven't found that the honor of my family has been impugned in any way. I left Atlanta for career opportunities and no other reason, so I'm surprised to hear him say that."

Today Michael says the relationship between his father and mother is good. "They're going to be friends forever," he says. "They still talk and they see each other. It's almost like nothing happened."

Julian Bond has reservations about his son's decision to enter politics. "I hope he doesn't stay in politics all his life, though it is a noble profession," he says.

But Michael talks as if he's in it for the long haul. He's going to run for office again in Atlanta. He has no plan to leave as his father did. "I told people since my loss, this is my hometown," he says. "I don't plan on leaving it. I love it and I'm going to be back in public life again."

James Forman Jr.
Son of James Forman Sr.

IT's A SUNNY SPRING DAY IN WASHINGTON, D.C., and James Forman Jr. is feeling good. His long legs are splayed out in front of a park bench as he chats about reaching kids that others deem unreachable.

James is talking about the success of the Maya Angelou Public Charter School, an institution he helped create for dropouts and juvenile offenders. He has taken a large group of his students to the park for a congratulatory field trip. Many are about to graduate.

He suddenly stops talking, spotting two of his students in the distance. "What in the world?" he says as his mouth opens in astonishment. "Oh my God."

In the middle of a softball game, two teenage girls have dropped their gloves and started fighting. By the time James rushes over, a crowd has gathered around the girls and pulled them apart as they continue to swipe and curse at one another. "We can't do nothing here without somebody starting a fight," says a girl, verging on tears.

After James helps calm his students down, he nonchalantly walks back to the bench and resumes talking about his charter school. "Self-esteem is a huge issue," he says. "That's what leads to so much of this 'fronting,' this false bravado."

That scene says much about what is distinctive about James. Self-esteem isn't an issue for him. He is the thirty-seven-year-old son of a famous civil rights activist, and a graduate of Brown University and Yale Law School. He served as a public defender for six years and as a judicial clerk for Supreme Court Justice Sandra Day O'Connor. With his credentials, he could land virtually any high-paying job he wanted—he has the name, the brains, and the background. Yet here he is in an inner-city park, breaking up a fight between two teenage girls. James's impromptu peacekeeping mission may not hold the glamour of leading a march or delivering a stirring speech, but working with troubled kids in forgotten, inner-city neighborhoods is part of extending the movement for him.

James is the son of James Forman Sr., a leader in the SNCC, the student shock troops who led the black voter registration campaigns in the South during the early 1960s. His mother is Constancia Romilly, another SNCC activist. (His brother, Chaka Forman, is profiled in Chapter 1.) Though separated by time and place, there are similarities between James's work and his father's. When his father campaigned for voters' rights in Mississippi, he had to convince black sharecroppers that their lives would improve if they pressed for the right to vote. James's challenge is persuading young blacks that their lives will improve if they do well in school.

It's a tough challenge. He has to confront not only their low self-esteem, but also the conflicting messages they receive in their neighborhoods, from their families, and, on occasion, from the police.

In a 2001 article on racial profiling he wrote for *The New Republic*, James described how many of his students were being stopped and searched by police who spotted them standing in front of the school. In one instance, a police officer charged into the school and wrestled a male student to the ground while drawing his gun, though no drugs were found on the student. "It's awfully hard to convince poor African American kids that discrimination isn't an obstacle, that authority must be respected, and that individual identity matters more than racial identity when experiences beyond school walls repeatedly contradict it," James wrote.

Yet some may argue that James's own success is proof that hard work pays off. When I bring this up, he dismisses it. "It's irrelevant to some of the kids that I work with that I went to Yale. That doesn't mean anything to their existence. What they need to know is how they can get out of neighborhoods where no one has a job. How can they get educated in a school system that is not serving them? How can they avoid a criminal justice system where, in D.C., one in three black males is in prison?"

James does not even invoke the success of his father's work in the civil rights movement as inspiration for his students. Conservative commentators have argued that a new generation of black youths is not prepared to take advantage of the open society created by the civil rights movement because they're too busy thinking of themselves as victims. "What do you call open?" James asks sharply. "Is the system open when they're born into a neighborhood where no one is working? It's not the child's fault that there are no industrial jobs left because they moved. It's not the child's fault he is in one of the worst school systems in the country. And then when they get out of the school system, if they somehow avoid being arrested, then the same job that didn't exist when they were born twenty years ago still isn't there."

A full forty years after his father fought for an open society in rural Mississippi, James says American society remains virtually closed. "It's open for the magnificent, the tiny few who can overcome those odds," he says. "Society should not be about setting up fifty-eight barriers and then if you can somehow miraculously overcome all of those barriers, they say, 'OK, now you can have a job, a decent place to live.'"

James got the idea for starting a charter school while he was working as a public defender for the District of Columbia. He held that job for five years. His office was located in the basement of an old building that looked like it should be condemned. Political posters adorned the walls and lawyers routinely worked through the weekend, often coming to work in jeans and shorts. When James's mother, Constancia, once visited, she told him, "This looks like a movement office."

James was startled by his mother's comment at the time but has since seen the truth of her statement. "Everyone who was there was doing it because they felt like it was us against the world," he says. "No one else cared about our clients. And we were the ones. For me it was the best job. It's so rare to find that in law. Lawyers are always complaining about job satisfaction—why am I doing what I'm doing? But there was none of that. You knew why you were doing it. You loved it. You worked seven days a week. But we were working with people like us who also loved it and that just carried you through day after day."

James became a public defender because he says he felt as if there were a whole group of blacks who had been left behind by the advances of the civil rights movement. Most were concentrated in the inner city. His idealism, though, was tested by the job. There were so many black youths getting churned up by the criminal justice system that the people who processed them—lawyers, cops, judges—became emotionally numb. "There's no way you can go to sleep at night doing the jobs that some of the people do in this system and some of these judges and prosecutors do," he says. "If you slow down enough to look at individuals, our failure as a society becomes too overwhelming. So they just process. They push. They look at charges and numbers. But they don't look at people."

James didn't want to follow that route. In 1995, mutual friends introduced him to David Domenici, the son of Republican U.S. Senator Pete Domenici. Like James, Domenici was a lawyer, but he had also worked as a middle school teacher and in investment banking. He, too, wanted to do more for kids. Together they created Project Soar, an after-school tutorial program and pizza delivery business for youths. The project was designed to teach youths how to run a legitimate business that would provide them with money.

James asked colleagues to send him students who had failed in public schools but still wanted to succeed. He also arranged for juvenile courts to send youths to Project Soar instead of reformatory school.

"People would say, 'This kid isn't doing well in school,' but when we looked around, there weren't any alternative schools that were available," he says. "People would say, 'This kid needs a good tutoring program or a good mentoring program,' and we'd look around, and it wouldn't be there."

The project grew so popular that Forman and Domenici realized they could do more. They created a foundation two years later (the See Forever Foundation), which led to the creation of the Maya Angelou Public Charter School. The foundation created a student technology center (where students teach computer skills to community residents) and a student-staffed catering service designed to teach job skills.

Yet the centerpiece of the See Forever Foundation is its charter school. The school stands in a four-story brick building in northwest Washington, D.C. It's surrounded by boarded-up homes and weed-choked lots. The area, which also contains some newer, spiffy brownstone homes, is being gentrified.

One reason students are often seen outside the building is because they spend so much time there. A typical class day lasts until 8:00 P.M., and students are required to work part-time at either the computer center or the catering service.

The school gives students plenty of reasons to succeed. At least 300 volunteer tutors work one-on-one with students. Parents are heavily involved; they tutor and sit in on the school's board meetings. Each one is called each day his or her child misses school. Students who become discipline problems are brought before a panel of students and teachers who determine if they should be expelled.

The students treat James like a big brother. Tall and bespectacled, he walks among them without a suit or tie, exchanging jokes and gently chiding them. Some adults who work with black kids try too hard to relate to them by clumsily talking slang or being too buddy-buddy. "Kids can spot a fake," James says. "As long as you are yourself, then they respect that. If you try to be somebody you're not, that's not going to work."

James grew up in Atlanta. His parents divorced when he was a child and his mother, who is white, took him to Atlanta because she wanted him to grow up around black people. The city had a reputation for having a strong, high-achieving black community. Growing up in the era of "Black Is Beautiful," James was sometimes teased by his classmates for being half-white, but it's not something that he's invested a lot of thought in. His parents taught him to define himself as black. For example, when he attended Brown he was puzzled to learn that there was a biracial support group on campus. "I was like, 'What in the world do these people have to talk about?' I just didn't get it, although I now understand more what people are talking about, in the sense of feeling like they are black but they are not fully accepted in the black community."

James says a person's social conscience, not skin color, is how most black people define an authentic black person. "The black community is a very welcoming community. The bottom line is what you are doing with your life. You can be as dark as you want to be but if people feel like you're doing something antithetical to the interests of the community and to social justice, they're going to say you're not black enough. They say Clarence Thomas isn't black enough. Thomas sure ain't light-skinned. And nobody challenges the blackness of Thurgood Marshall."

What shaped James's worldview was what he calls "the family business": civil rights activism. During visits with his father and talks with his mother, James says he and his younger brother were constantly told that they had a responsibility to create a society that offers people more opportunities than they had. "I grew up in an environment where human rights and equality and opportunity were things you heard about at breakfast, after dinner, and every time in-between."

The Forman men together: James Forman Jr. right; James Forman Sr., middle; Chaka Forman, left.

Courtesy of Chaka Forman

Since he started the Maya Angelou School, James has steadily gained media attention for his efforts and for his civil rights lineage. But he doesn't believe he's doing anything extraordinary. "I'm much more impressed by people who don't have my background who do the work I do," he says. "To me, it seems like the obvious. I grew up being raised on that's what mattered. It didn't require leaps of imagination. I didn't have to get outside of myself."

On the day of his field trip to the park, James's father, James Forman Sr., shows up at the school. Now seventy-six and battling colon cancer, he looks markedly different from the burly civil rights activist who once stormed the pulpit of the famed Riverside Church in New York City during a Sunday morning service to read his demands for a Black Manifesto. Today he is rail thin and talks in a raspy, strained voice.

"He was always more soft-spoken than the clips I've seen," James says. "His personality is totally different from the descriptions of people who knew him back in the day. The only personality I've known is the one I've seen."

Father and son greet each other in the lobby of James's school like colleagues. They are polite to one another, but there's a formality to their exchanges—no warm embrace or easy smiles. James says he is much closer to his mother than his father.

When I ask him if his father is proud of him, James pauses and thinks about the question for a while. "Well, let me put it like this. I know that he's proud of me. Has he said the words 'I'm proud of you'? I couldn't say. But I know that he is just based on how he carries himself, how he talks."

When I ask the elder Forman how he feels about his son's work, he says it's part of the ongoing work of the movement. "I'm very happy. It's not a question of being proud. I think he's working very hard trying to make it possible for some people to live a better life."

One dream of some civil rights leaders from Forman's generation was that of the Beloved Community, best articulated by King in his "I Have a Dream" speech. It was based on the idea that Americans of different races could live in harmony with one another.

At its essence, the Maya Angelou School exists to realize that dream, James says. He still believes in the importance of integration but says many whites seem to be uninterested in the concept. When, for example, he was growing up in Atlanta, virtually no whites would attend black public schools, even if those schools had well-established academic reputations. "There is so much self-imposed segregation, particularly from the white community, and isolation on the part of a lot of our kids that's not really self-imposed, but it's imposed by society. They live in these neighborhoods because they can't afford to live anywhere else. No one wants them in their school. That is a problem."

Racial isolation extends to even the most progressive social circles in which he travels, he says. "I am continually stunned by reasonably progressive people who basically vote Democratic, people I've talked with over the years and share a lot of core values with. And I go to their engagement parties, their weddings, their baby showers, their houses, and I will be the only black person there."

James hopes for a day when many blacks will be able to make the leap from the inner city to mainstream America. Then there would be no need for a Maya Angelou School. "As long as we're living in that state of isolation," he says, "there's going to be a lot of ignorance about one another, and there's going to be a lot of prejudice and stereotypes, and there's not going to be a lot of working together. We need to overcome that in our country and we need to overcome it internationally."

Julie Guyot
Daughter of Lawrence Guyot Jr.

"Sa-aat." The Cambodian woman used the Khmer word for *beautiful* as she caressed Julie's lightly shaded arm, stroking it in appreciation. Julie, the child of an interracial couple who met during the civil rights movement, eased her arm out of the grasp of the elderly woman whose skin displayed the blotchy evidence of an attempt at whitening.

The woman's comment brought back some ugly memories for Julie. Her parents were in *Jet* magazine in 1969 when they broke Mississippi's antimiscegenation law to marry one another. Both were activists in SNCC who risked their lives when they decided to live together in Mississippi during the mid-1960s. They were, as her father announced, "integrationists" in their personal and political lives.

Julie grew up determined not to carry the biracial banner. She thought too many biracial kids whined about identity. She defined herself as black, end of story. No "tragic mulatto" role for her.

Yet Julie discovered that she couldn't escape the color caste system. She traveled halfway around the world but still met people who called her a nigger. She encountered the same obsession with skin color in Asia, Europe, and South America that her parents had fought against in the Mississippi of the 1960s.

Southeast Asia was the worst. She traveled alone to Cambodia in 2002 to write freelance articles and work with victims of the region's sex trade industry. She quickly noticed that people were fixated on being lighter. Creams used to bleach the skin were big business. The country's news programs and soap operas were full of light-skinned people. Dark skin was the mark of a peasant. The color caste system even infiltrated the region's sex trade industry: Vietnamese call girls with light skin commanded higher prices.

"I'd always naively assumed that black folks had the market share of color consciousness—that it was an 'us' thing—not realizing how much other cultures value the same shady business," Julie wrote later in her journal, describing the encounter with the Cambodian woman. "I was embarrassed for her, for her inability to see her own toffee beauty."

In his "I Have a Dream" speech, Martin Luther King Jr. sketched a vision of America in which people of various races would "sit at the table of brotherhood." King's vision of this "Beloved Community" galvanized both white and black activists. In places as diverse as rural Mississippi, Alabama, and Chicago, black and white activists worked, suffered, and died next to one another. Some even fell in love and had children.

Julie, now thirty-two, is the daughter of one such couple. Lawrence Guyot, who has been featured in the *Eyes on the Prize* documentary and numerous civil rights books, is a black Creole native of Louisiana. Monica Guyot is Jewish. Julie's dual heritage is displayed in her café-au-lait complexion and her curly hair.

No one has counted how many biracial children came out of the movement, but interracial couples were not uncommon. Movement leaders such as Ernest Green of the Little Rock Nine, James Forman, and James Bevel all had biracial children.

In some circles, children such as these are seen as the vanguard of King's Beloved Community. The Harvard University sociologist Nathan Glazer suggested that interracial marriages offer the best chance of creating a successful multiracial society in the United States. That notion sounds utopian to some, but people in the United States seem to be getting more comfortable with interracial couples. Biracial celebrities like golfer Tiger Woods and actress Halle Berry even make being biracial seem cool.

Such talk, however, leaves Julie unmoved. I meet her in the Washington, D.C., brownstone she shares with her family. When I bring up the subject of being biracial, both she and her younger brother, Lawrence Guyot III, chuckle. They define themselves as black, not biracial or anything else. "Lawrence and I never discuss it," she says. "We just roll our eyes in disgust and move on."

Julie Guyot as an infant with her mother, Monica, and her father, Lawrence Guyot. The Guyots made national news and risked their lives when they had Julie.

Lawrence Guyot III possesses facial features that are so ambiguous that he was often mistaken for a Thai when he lived in Thailand. But he won't take the Tiger Woods route and call himself a "cablinasian" (a mixture of white, black, Native American, and Asian). "People say, 'Did you choose to be white or did you choose to be black?' Even if you didn't want to be black, the law would say if you got black blood, you're black. And you are. Deal with it. Be proud of who you are."

Julie says interracial couples who raise their kids as biracial do them a disservice. They don't prepare them for encounters with racism. "They deny them confidence. That's wrong to cheapen a child's experience like that." She isn't sure she agrees with the argument that interracial marriages promote tolerance.

What infuriates Julie is any kind of talk that hints that biracial people are somehow special or more desirable. Once, in college, a man she was falling for told her that they could make beautiful babies. End of relationship. "I realized he wasn't looking at me," she says. "He was looking at these components: light skin, light eyes, 'good hair,' that kind of thing. That disappointed me. I thought he was a man."

Julie and her brother even have their doubts about integration. When I ask them if they think it's still an important goal, they exchange bemused glances before answering. "It sounds like an old-fashioned word," Julie says.

Her brother, using an argument that segregationists once used, says: "I'm not for forced integration. When you talk about mandatory—saying, I'm going to send my kids to this type of school—I don't believe in that. If you force people, they're going to inherently reject that on some level."

Their father, Lawrence Jr., says he taught his children that they were black so that they would be prepared to deal with racism. He describes the successful campaign to create a separate category for biracial people on the U.S. census as a "reach for political oblivion." "Political districts and the allocation of money for programs are often based on race," he says.

"It's divisive and it's more costly politically to black people," he says. "If race were in fact a nullity and if we lived in a country purely devoid of racism and if about ten other things were to occur, I would then give some legitimacy to this escapism."

Lawrence Guyot Jr. still believes that integration is vital for America's future. "The absence of integration is really antithetical to fulfilling the possibilities of all of us," he says. "I've watched how groups have to demonize another group of individuals to feel that they're on the rise. It's unethical and a waste of time."

Monica Guyot says integration isn't as important to her as making sure people have a decent standard of living. "He talks about race all the time; I don't," she says, looking at her husband, who had joined her and Julie at their dining room table. "When I think of us, I don't think of us as a black couple, an integrationist couple, whatever. I think that this is the man I love, the man I respect, the man I like, and he's my pain in the ass but I love him anyway. I don't look at him and say I've married an African American man."

After Lawrence and Monica married, they literally made national news when they moved back to Mississippi in the mid-1960s to live together while working for SNCC. "Everybody knew where we were staying," Lawrence Guyot Jr. says. "Everyone knew we were together. It was just part of the fabric. In order to do anything in Mississippi, you must first deal with the question of fear. You either transcend it or move beyond it. And that's what you did."

Monica Guyot says they were too exhilarated by their work and one another to abandon their relationship. "I'd get a phone call: 'Tell that nigger, Guyot, that tonight's his last day.' I'd say OK. I'd call him wherever he was and say, 'Well, you got another threat.' He'd say, 'OK, I'll see you tonight.'"

Monica says she ran into white people who called her white trash and told her she was going to hell. Many blacks objected to the Guyots' union too, but weren't hateful. "I luvvv black folks," Monica says. "They're so much nicer. They would say to him, we don't like you going with this white woman, but if you're going to go with her, at least do the honest thing and marry her."

Lawrence Guyot Jr., now sixty-four, works in the office of a government-run after-school program in Washington, D.C., and is a leader in the campaign to grant D.C. statehood. Monica Guyot, now 66, is the executive director of a child development center there. Their son is an entrepreneur who owns his own computer company.

<hr>

As Julie talks with her family at their Washington home, their closeness is palpable. After her frequent travels around the world, she has taken a break to stay with her parents. The family seems to relish their time together. They laugh often and easily with one another. And they love to debate. Everybody seems to have an opinion. Sitting at their table is like listening to a Sunday morning political talk show.

Knowing what her parents went through shapes the way she approaches relationships, Julie says. "I know what commitment is because of my parents. They don't agree on anything. They have an active, vigorous dialogue but they respect and like each other so much."

Julie's parents have shaped her in another way. She is a restless activist, literally wandering the world looking for a cause. Often, as in her travels in Cambodia, she prefers to work away from big Western aid agencies and find smaller groups in the country to help. Most of her work centers on helping children or educating poor women. "The only job I've ever had is that I help people," she says. "I've been too busy living to build a career. I just keep moving. Other people want to establish themselves. But I don't think that's my focus."

In 1998 Julie joined the Peace Corps. She had worked as a White House intern and at various community development programs, but, like her parents, she wanted to join a cause. "I just wanted to leap out there to see what I would accomplish," she says.

When she first applied to the Peace Corps, Julie encountered a situation she would run into again overseas: stereotyping over her color. The Peace Corps recruiter wanted her to go to the Caribbean or Africa but she insisted on Russia. She wanted to get away from the black/white racial worldview.

But she couldn't. "In Russian, the word for a black person is, literally, *nigger*," she says. "It doesn't have the same stigma. They don't know what it means. They would say, "Michael Jordan, cool nigger.' I would go, 'Ah, let me explain.'"

Julie taught English in Russia. But she grew restless working in the bureaucracy of the Peace Corps. She wanted to work without the safety net of an established group. Someone told her about a group in the former Soviet republic of Georgia that worked with homeless kids. When Julie moved there to work and live with street kids in a homeless shelter, she was awed by their resiliency. "Everything is against them," she

Courtesy of Julie Guyot

The Guyots all together. Lawrence III, bottom, followed by Julie, Monica, and Lawrence Jr.

says. "They have no family name in a society where that carries all too much weight. They don't have their health. They're all stunted. I'm looking at a twelve-year-old who I would have sworn was eight. Kids have been sexually abused and sold off by their parents. Yet these kids are capable of love, learning, affection. They have opinions. They're survivors."

Julie was also surprised to find echoes of black history in the story of Georgia. That region of the Soviet Union was known for preserving its own language and cultural identity in the face of often violent persecution. Some citizens could identify with the plight of black Americans, as Julie discovered one day when she entered a store.

A young Georgian, spotting her tan complexion and her bouffant curls, called over to her. "He just looked over at me and he puts up the black power sign and says, 'Angela Davis.' He freaked me out in such a beautiful way. I made the symbol back at him and I went on my way."

Julie says she also loves to nestle in other countries to learn about herself. Each challenge she meets while traveling and each person she encounters somehow refines her. "If you keep moving you'll find that the only thing you end up carrying is yourself. I'm pushing myself to see who I am in all these different kinds of situations."

But what she won't ever be is an exotic symbol of race-mixing for the new millennium. "I've encountered dark-skinned or mixed people," she says, "but I don't present myself as anything but Julie."

Andrew "Bo" Young III
Son of Andrew Young

Andrew Young has been Martin Luther King's confidant, an ambassador to the United Nations, and a two-term mayor of Atlanta. He has received countless honors during four decades of public service. But there's one thing missing from his resume that his son, Andrew "Bo" Young III, is determined to accomplish.

Andrew Young didn't get rich.

"He brought over $90 billion to Atlanta," Bo says of his father. "All these white folks got rich and they're smiling and saying what great friends they are with 'Andy,' but they aren't offering any free membership at clubs or any board memberships. They continue to leech off of him and just give him a pat on the back."

Bo recalls a group of business leaders gathering to give his father a going-away gift after he ended his second term as mayor of Atlanta. "They gave him two cars and said, 'Nigger, here go two cars. Goodbye. We got no job for you. Nobody wants to hire you. We ain't got time for you.'"

Bo, a stocky thirty-one-year-old entrepreneur with a booming baritone, asks why white folks should have all the money. He wants to become a millionaire. "I want to integrate the money," he says.

Being a civil rights leader may make you a hero, but it won't pay the bills. As I talked to children of famous movement activists, many complained that their families didn't reap any financial rewards. Many of them said that they had watched people profit from their parents' work in the movement for years. They wanted to know when some of those profits were going to come their way.

Bo doesn't talk about making money off his father's name. He's not, for example, trying to market his father's image or speeches. But a life

84

like that of his father, in which a person toils in public service while others get rich, is not something that appeals to him. He has his eyes on a different prize.

"Bo always said as a little boy, 'I want to be rich. My sisters have all these degrees and they're all broke. Nobody in this family has got any money,'" Andrew Young Sr., now seventy-two, says. "I've always had enough money. I never tried to make money. I turned down opportunities to make money. I just think that's obscene."

But for Bo, acquiring wealth is the next stage of the movement. Bo sees himself as a compassionate capitalist. He's not that different from his father, he says. "We have the same goal, to feed the hungry, clothe the naked, and shelter the homeless."

But Bo needs to make money to fulfill that New Testament command. He says he wants to be rich to create jobs for the less fortunate, much like former NBA great Magic Johnson has done, by creating jobs through his business empire.

Quoting the billionaire investor Warren Buffett, Bo says being rich "is just a report card in capitalism to show how well you're doing. In America, you're judged by your economic and financial ability. Money is a necessary evil."

Bo is the founder and CEO of Young Solutions, a company that manufactures envelopes, business forms, and printing supplies for Fortune 500 companies. He has ownership interests in five other small companies. "We have small budgets but big dreams," he says.

I meet Bo in his Atlanta home, which is filled with *Black Enterprise* magazines, *Golfing for Dummies*, and pictures of him with his family nestled among African artwork. In person, Bo is as blunt as a punch in the face, occasionally profane, and invariably confident. He has three older sisters, but no brothers. His mother, Jean Childs Young, died of cancer in 1994.

Bo's bluntness is far different from the public image of his father, who was known as the moderate, the diplomat, in King's inner circle. As vice president of the SCLC, Andrew Young Sr. was often called to mediate between the strong personalities in the SCLC and the white business leaders the group encountered during their nonviolent campaigns in the South. Today he is the chairman of Good Works International, an Atlanta-based consulting firm that works with corporations and foreign governments. In this job, Young drums up business through meetings with prime ministers, presidents, and corporate leaders from around the world. But people still think of him primarily as a civil rights activist and a politician.

Courtesy of Bo Young

A youthful Andrew "Bo" Young with his father, Andrew Young Sr.

People often ask Bo if he's going to run for office as his father did. "I hate that," Bo says. "No way. Is that all you think I'm good for, to kiss babies and to help everybody else get rich?"

I couldn't imagine Bo kissing babies on the campaign trail given his past. His pugnacious nature often made the Atlanta headlines while his father was mayor. When he was a high school and college student, Bo was arrested at various times for possessing a small amount of marijuana, drunk driving, and weapon and alcohol possession charges. In another case, three Washington, D.C., police officers were indicted for assaulting Bo after they were summoned to a party. After the assault, Bo conceded that he was developing a bad-boy reputation. "I know in Atlanta I'm not considered the perfect child role model, and they have all this stuff about a politician's son gone bad," he told the *Atlanta Constitution* right after the incident. "What goes on with me has nothing to do with my father. I've been in a lot of bad situations that really weren't my fault."

As a teenager, Bo says, part of his trouble sprang from rebelling against people's expectations. Teachers told him he should be a leader. He couldn't tell who his real friends were. He was constantly stopped by people in public who wanted to talk about his father, politics, or his own behavior. "People would come up to me and say, 'You're embarrassing your father. You need to set a better example for other kids.' This would literally come from people stopping me in the mall, in the grocery store, or at the movie theater." A few teachers empathized with the pressures he faced being the mayor's son, but they were the minority. "Everybody wanted me to be Andrew Young's kid. Nobody wanted me to just be Bo."

Yet a part of him reveled in shattering people's expectations. "I went out of my way to make sure I could be as bad a kid as I could be," he says. "I just didn't want to be identified with being the prissy good kid. I was already light-skinned. Then my dad was famous. I didn't want to get caught up in that punk category."

Courtesy of Bo Young

Bo Young with his mother, the late Jean Childs Young, and his father, Andrew Young.

He says he was never personally embarrassed by all the notoriety he received. "When I would go to school, I was a hero," he says. "Everybody at school was impressed with the fact that I was such a bad kid."

At home, Bo says, his father refused to blame him for his run-ins with the law. Nor did he ever say that Bo was embarrassing him. Instead he told Bo to watch his temper and not worry about what people said.

Bo says he was relieved when his father refused to criticize him. "That would have made him just as bad as those other people. If he would expect that out of me, then that would have given other people the right to expect that out of me as opposed to just allowing me to be a kid."

Bo says he never got any lectures from his father or exhortations to be like him. At times, though, he admits that he wanted his father to lean on him more. "I wanted some direction. I wanted him to tell me what he wanted me to be. He didn't have any interest in trying to tell me that. He wanted to let God steer my life so I could find my own course."

Andrew Young Sr. says part of the reason he didn't lecture his son was guilt. He knew that his celebrity made his son a target for the media and police.

I talk to him from his office in downtown Atlanta. "I felt like what was happening to him was my fault," he says. "If he had not been my son, he never would have gotten in the paper."

Young Sr. says that part of his light touch with his son was also influenced by his own relationship with his father. Young Sr.'s father pushed and manipulated him into choosing a career as a dentist. Young Sr. pursued dentistry just to please his father. When he decided to enter the ministry, his father never got over the disappointment. "I didn't want to put my children through that," says Young Sr. "I never wanted to force my children to follow in my footsteps. I wanted them to find their own way." And he allowed them to do so by not making demands on them. "I let them do anything they wanted to do instead of pushing them."

What he did try to teach his son was to be less argumentative in his encounters with police. He told Bo he had to learn how to express himself in a nonthreatening manner. "He never felt he had to learn it," Young Sr. says of his son. "I was taught a kind of nonviolent approach almost from two or three years old because we lived in a white neighborhood. My parents taught me to deal with an unjust, racist world and to understand that the world was sick, not you. But you're very careful when you're dealing with sick people. I didn't do that with my kids. I almost brought them up to believe that the world was fair and that we had changed things significantly. And it's not, and it's still sick."

Young Sr. was also patient with his son because he remembers how he himself was as a young man. People tend to think of civil rights leaders as people who always had it together—even when they were young. "When I started in the movement in Thomasville, Georgia, I was twenty-two years old," Young Sr. says. "I was just as confused and just as screwed up as most twenty-two-year-olds. When I hooked up with Martin Luther King Jr., we were all struggling to figure out who we were and what we ought to do. The only difference is that we stuck together and we did the right thing at the right time."

Young Sr. says his son may think he should have more money, but he's doing fine in that department. A glance at the location of his office is evidence enough: it's in one of the fanciest office districts in downtown Atlanta. Young Sr. sits on the board of directors for corporations such as Delta Airlines, Host Marriott Corporation, and Cox Communications.

"I've always made enough money," Andrew says. "I've been able to live within means, whether it was making $190 a month as a pastor, or now, when we're doing quite well. But I'm doing what I want to do and I'm happy, and money comes with that."

Bo, however, doesn't understand why his father never took advantage of opportunities to make more money, even when businesspeople offered him generous sums for various projects after he left the mayor's office. "They offered a few times to give him some money, but he turned him down," Bo says. "He didn't want anything for it. And he doesn't have any bitterness about it or regret it."

Young Sr. says he's told his son that he should figure out what he wants to do with his life and the money will come. "He doesn't want to wait," he says. "Bo wants to be a millionaire by the time he's thirty or at least thirty-five. Not only do I not understand it, I don't believe in it, and it's somewhat offensive to me. I don't think you seek money. I think you first seek the Kingdom of God and all these things will be added unto you."

Young Sr. says he wants to see his children living successful Christian lives, not successful American lives. "To live a successful American life, you conform to the existing situation, regardless of what it is," he says. "I wouldn't do that. I was never a good student. Everything that made me a bad student made me a good adult and a leader. I always challenged authority. I always questioned people's opinions. I always tried to think for myself."

Andrew Young sees the same trait in his son. "I never want him to lose that, even if it means going to jail or getting killed," he says.

Bo thinks now that he can do both—live the Christian life his father wants and be rich. He plans to build a career that answers a question that was once posed by King: what's the use of integrating a lunch counter if you can't afford to buy a hamburger? Bo plans on buying the building that holds the lunch counter.

"Martin Luther King says you can't have people isolated on these lonely islands of poverty in this sea of prosperity," he says. "The money needs integrating."

3

Children of the Icons

BOTH WERE THE SONS OF PREACHERS. Both were thirty-nine years old when they were assassinated. And both were so selfless that they left their families with virtually no money at the time of their deaths.

Martin Luther King Jr. and El-Hajj Malik El-Shabazz—known as Malcolm X—are the two iconic figures to emerge from the civil rights movement. No other leaders from that era command the same respect. King is the only American of color to have a national holiday named after him. His "I Have a Dream" speech ranks alongside the Gettysburg Address as a classic American document. Malcolm X's greatest sermon was the transformation of his life. At a time when more black American men are confined to jail than are attending college, Malcolm X's evolution from a petty criminal to a civil rights giant reaches people in places that even King's soaring oratory cannot.

No look at the children of the leading figures from the civil rights movement would be complete without the voices of King's and Malcolm X's children. Given their prominence, their stories may be more familiar to most readers. Martin Luther King III, for example, is a public figure who travels the lecture circuit and heads a civil rights group. Ilyasah

Shabazz recently wrote a book about what it was like to grow up as the daughter of Malcolm X.

Yet there are sides to their story that they have seldom discussed publicly. King defends his family's aggressive attempts to profit from their father's image. And Shabazz talks about her feelings concerning Nation of Islam leader Minister Louis Farrakhan, who is widely believed to have helped orchestrate her father's murder.

No other children have such larger-than-life parents. Each had the guidance of a strong mother, too. But both ultimately had to find their own way.

Martin Luther King III
Son of Reverend Martin Luther King Jr.

MARTIN LUTHER KING III LEANS BACK in his creaky office chair as his voice takes on a dreamy, detached tone. Once again, someone is asking him to be "Little Marty."

I've just asked the son of Martin Luther King Jr. how he coped with the loss of his father. Sighing, he talks about his memories of his boyhood; the times he ached for his father's presence, and the mission his mother assigned him after his father was assassinated.

"I was told that I was the man of the house," King says. "So at eleven years old, I was trying to fulfill that mission, whatever I thought it was, not necessarily knowing what it was. I was concerned about closing up the blinds, making sure doors were locked. Whenever I'm in the house today, I still do the same things. . . ."

Suddenly something odd happens. King snaps out of his reverie. He straightens up in his chair, clears his throat, and abruptly changes the subject. Little Marty disappears. "You know, we're living in a very interesting time," he tells me. "The suicide rate is going up; homicides are going up. I was in Europe the other day and I was in one of those airports. . . ."

That moment encapsulates the dilemma in King's life. He wants to talk about his future, but his past keeps intruding. He's constantly asked to relive the most anguished moment of his life—the moment when he lost his father and his childhood.

Martin is the president of the Southern Christian Leadership Conference (SCLC), the same organization his father led when it was at the vanguard of the civil rights movement in the 1950s and 1960s. The SCLC, led by black clergy, directed most of the movement's most celebrated campaigns. In cities such as Birmingham and Selma, Alabama, they reversed more than a century's worth of segregationist policy through acts of mass civil disobedience.

Those glory days are constant reminders in the SCLC's office near downtown Atlanta. The inside of the office in which I meet King looks like a civil rights shrine: paintings and portraits of Martin Luther King Jr. and placard-carrying demonstrators line the walls. On one wall hangs a series of portraits of the SCLC's past presidents: King Jr.; Ralph Abernathy Jr.; Joseph Lowery; and now Martin. Martin's portrait is the smallest one.

In person, forty-seven-year-old Martin is a big man with a soft, boyish voice. Broad-shouldered, thick in the torso, with a salt-and-pepper beard, he is polite and deferential.

He is the eldest of King's sons. His older sister, Yolanda, is an actress. His younger sister, Bernice, who seems to have inherited the electrifying speaking ability of her father, is a minister. His younger brother, Dexter, oversees the licensing of his father's image and usage fees for his speeches, and has moved to Malibu, California, to break into the entertainment industry.

But none of the other King children have stepped so publicly into their father's role. When Martin was elected president of the SCLC in 1998, SCLC leaders openly rhapsodized about the symbolism of getting King's eldest son and namesake to infuse new life into the organization.

"When Martin comes to the table, he brings more when he sits down than most of us do, by him being a King," Reverend R. N. Gooden, a SCLC board member, told an *Atlanta Constitution* reporter at the time. "He brings the name and he has the authority to use that name. That is the reason he was brought in."

Martin started his SCLC presidency off strong. He held a series of national hearings on racial profiling. He also talked about transforming the SCLC's forty-member board of trustees, adding young members as well as whites and Latinos.

But in 2001 SCLC's board chairman suspended Martin for seven days and threatened to fire him. He claimed Martin's lack of work ethic, frequent stints away from the group's Atlanta headquarters, and inability to raise money led to the suspension.

Martin was reinstated by the SCLC's board later that year. But today, he says, there's still tension between him and some members of the

Demonstrators Lonnie King, on left, an unidentified
woman, and Martin Luther King Jr. are taken to a police
car after being arrested for a sit-in protest at Rich's
department store in Atlanta in 1960.

board. "Many of these men wanted us to go back to our glory days when
my father was one of the few leaders out there on the scene," he says.
But Martin says that people forget that after his father led the Montgomery Bus Boycott, he spent four years marshalling his resources
before embarking on his next major campaign. Some SCLC board
members want another Montgomery campaign. Martin says tactics
have to change with time. "I don't think they even understand that," he
says. "These are people—some of them are seventy-five, eighty years
old—they want to see another quick victory as in the glory days. The

world is different these days. Not everything you're going to take on today is going to be a national story. They want to see us in somebody's face, telling them off."

Martin was never known as a confrontational person, says Michael Ross, his friend since childhood. "He's never been a kind of boisterous person that always felt like he had to be leader of the pack. He didn't have that need to be recognized. He didn't have this arrogant drum major instinct." Ross describes Martin as an ordinary guy with an extraordinary name. He loves basketball (friends say he has a good jump shot), does a great imitation of Richard Pryor, and likes listening to contemporary jazz and gospel.

"He's smart, sensitive," says Andrew Young, an SCLC board member and Martin's mentor. "He's very loving, courageous, and sacrificial."

Yet Martin has not carved out a distinctive career. He has never distinguished himself as a student or a public official. He graduated in 1979 from Morehouse College, his father's alma mater, with "about a 2.9" grade-point average on a 4.0 scale. His major was political science.

He was elected in 1986 to the Fulton County Commission, a seven-member board that governs one of the largest counties in the metropolitan Atlanta area. One of his proudest moments as a politician came the next year, when he introduced a law requiring the county government to hire an equal percentage of women and minorities when hiring contractors.

But that achievement was eclipsed by one of Martin's most humiliating moments as a public official. In 1993, Martin resigned his position to run for the commission's chair. He was opposed by Mitch Skandalakis, a relatively unknown white candidate and political novice. Martin held a commanding lead with less than a week to go in the election. But he was absent from the city for nearly a third of the five-week campaign. Then it was disclosed that the Internal Revenue Service had slapped more than $200,000 in liens on Martin over disputed business expenses. Martin settled the dispute with a $150,000 family loan.

Coretta Scott King, wearing hat and gloves, and her four children (to her right) view the body of her husband, slain civil rights leader Martin Luther King Jr., in Atlanta on April 7, 1968. The children from left: Yolanda, twelve; Bernice, five; Martin III, eleven; and Dexter, seven.

But the damage was done. Martin lost the election. The eldest son and namesake of Martin Luther King Jr. couldn't even win a hometown election against an inexperienced white opponent.

At the time, Robert Holmes, a Clark Atlanta University professor and local politician, delivered an assessment of Martin that has followed him ever since. "He was never viewed as a leader in the sense that he could inspire people, that he could make tough decisions, and that he had a vision," Holmes told an *Atlanta Constitution* reporter.

Yet Martin still had his name. After his defeat, Martin toured the country as a public speaker, making as much as $100,000 in 1990 on speaking engagements alone. (The agency that handles his speeches, Lordly & Dame, refused to disclose how much Martin is currently earning as a speaker.)

His last foray into local politics took place in 1999, when Georgia's governor appointed Martin to the Georgia Regional Transportation Authority (GRTA), an agency that handles transportation growth for the state. Martin missed five of the twelve GRTA meetings and would have been removed from the board had he missed another. He resigned from the board, citing his responsibilities as the head of the SCLC.

Martin admits that he's not yet found the role that would capture all of his passion. His father found it, but he himself is still looking. He plucks an example from his playground basketball days to illustrate his point. "I could shoot a bit," he says, smiling at the memory. "But one of my friends was so passionate about it. He'd holler at me, 'Shoot, King. You're not hustling!' And I was just going up and down the court. My position was if we lost, it wasn't dreadful. I'm not going to kill me out on the basketball court. In one sense, maybe that's how I think about life. I feel that I'm going to push as much as I need to push. But I'm not sure I found the one thing that I'll push so much that it might cause death."

But people want Martin to push more. They want passion. They want inspiration. When he goes to speak at SCLC events, colleagues say, people light up with awe at the chance to meet King's namesake and son. They want to hear his father again.

"Everybody wants him to be Martin Luther King," Young says. "And he's not going to be Martin Luther King. He's going to be Martin III."

Even the reporters who periodically interview him seem disappointed that he's just a regular guy. In a GQ magazine profile, the writer portrayed him as a distracted man-child who's not fit for his role. In another article a writer, after meeting Martin, wrote about a childlike vulnerability that peeks through his interaction with others. "He is soft-spoken and seems shy. Doesn't easily make eye contact. Perhaps he worries that if you look into the eyes of Martin King III, you'll only find Little Marty."

When this quote is read back to him, Martin listens impassively, hands clasped, nodding in a businesslike manner. He doesn't seem annoyed at all. "That's not accurate," he finally says. "The shy part is accurate. I've always been shy. But the rest, I would have a difference of opinion about."

He's also been described as a mama's boy because he still lives at home with his mother—in the same Atlanta house that his father purchased. Martin says he stays home with his mother to protect her.

I asked him if he ever gets hurt by depictions of him in the media, and just a trace of hurt creeps into his voice before it vanishes. "Sure, of course," he says. "You can't be a human and not be impacted. It's a vicious attack that's unwarranted."

Martin doesn't seem to have a passion for celebrity either. When he goes out in public, he's constantly stopped by people wanting pictures or an autograph. A ten-minute trip to the supermarket can easily stretch into an hour. The attention can be draining. He tacks on an extra half-hour to his public errands because he knows he's going to have to accommodate well-wishers.

"This is every day," he says. "No matter where I go in this country. It's not bad in all cities. It's wonderful for people to come up. . . . The only problem is when it comes to the group. They're almost like a herd."

In the beginning, Martin felt odd having people clamor for his autograph. "I used to have a problem with signing because I'm like, 'What do I need to sign for? I'm inheriting all of this because of my dad. I didn't see my signature as that significant.' "

If Martin doesn't like the attacks or the celebrity that comes with his name, then why invite more of that by taking the very job his father once had? Martin says it goes back to the sense of obligation that comes with his name. It's the same reason he took on the duties of closing the blinds as a boy in his home—it was the mission that was thrust upon him whether he was ready for it or not. "I think it's important to be here to continue the process. I think my objective is to carry the legacy forward to the next level."

Michael Ross says Martin is maturing into a role that he has never sought. "At first, he may have been reluctant to be a leader. But because of his sense of commitment and compassion, he feels that this is his legacy that he was born to fulfill."

Andrew Young, however, isn't so sure that Martin has matured into his role as a civil rights leader. "He's letting himself be pushed into it. He hasn't decided who he is yet or who he wants to be."

Although Martin says that his father's legacy casts an "awesome shadow," he doesn't torture himself with comparisons. "I never saw myself trying to compete. I knew from the beginning that I can't. I never even had that notion."

Martin's memories of his father, who was away from home most of the time, are few. He remembers riding his bicycle with his father, tossing a softball, and kissing and hugging him when he would return home from his travels.

Martin says his family's faith taught him to accept the loss of his father. It's the same faith he and his siblings leaned on when their grandmother, Alberta Williams King, was shot to death by Marcus Wayne Chenault in 1974 while she was playing the organ at her church in Atlanta. "The healing process can take a lifetime. We were kind of taught, and I accepted this as a kid, that Daddy was going home to live

Courtesy of the Southern Christian Leadership Conference

Martin Luther King III, right, sits with the man he replaced as president of the Southern Christian Leadership Conference, Reverend Joseph Lowery.

with God, that he had been a good and faithful servant and that God rewards those who serve Him. I was also taught not to dislike the evil-doer, but the evil act. That's what I embraced. I never thought about hating James Earl Ray or Marcus Wayne Chenault."

But the grief would swell up to the surface at odd times when he became older. "When I was growing up and I wanted to talk to my father to get advice, and no one was there, it hit then. It hit me when my mom would say, 'Your father would be so proud of you today.' That was painful."

So were the dreams he would sometimes have. In these dreams, his father was still alive. Nothing had happened to him. "On one or two occasions he was present, looking over me, making sure I was safe."

As Martin talks about his father, he fidgets in his chair and his voice becomes detached. The early loss of his father, the weight of his last name, his shyness—these things made it difficult for him to make friends growing up. "Most of my friends I've known for at least twenty years," he says. "There are not really any new people that have really become close, at least thus far. I'm introduced to new people from time to time, but that's not really a personal scenario."

As he moves toward middle age, Martin is still alone. He says he wants to get married, but his constant traveling prevents him from cultivating a relationship. There are also emotional reasons why he and his siblings have stayed single. "Most of us have devoted our lives to our work. We had to go through a number of things, like the healing. It's hard to bring individuals into your circle who generally cannot totally understand your circumstances. It doesn't mean that there's not somebody that exists but maybe up to this point, none of us have met them."

There are some people who can relate to his loss. Martin says he and his siblings have befriended the children of Malcolm X and Medgar Evers. Over the years, he's met several of them at civil rights events and they've stayed in touch. But they've never talked about the loss of their fathers with one another. "I don't know how they feel conceptually. We've been together several times, but we never talked about those issues."

One issue that Martin has been open about is his belief that James Earl Ray wasn't responsible for his father's murder. For years he and his siblings have suspected that the murder was the result of an elaborate conspiracy. They thought that their suspicions were confirmed when Dexter King, Martin's younger brother, met William Pepper, a lawyer who wrote a book about a conspiracy between the federal government and organized crime to murder his father.

Pepper persuaded Dexter King that the U.S. government had formed a special military hit team that killed his father and used Ray as a fall guy. Before James Earl Ray died in 1998, Dexter King visited Ray to publicize his family's wish that Ray receive a new trial. He met Ray in a medical detention ward (Ray's liver was failing and he was near death) and heard his father's convicted killer again claim his innocence.

Although Ray died in 1998 without being exonerated for the crime, the King family lodged a civil wrongful-death suit against Lloyd Jowers, a Memphis barkeep who they said was a coconspirator in their father's death. The trial ended in 1999, when a Memphis jury declared that King's assassination was part of a larger conspiracy, rather than committed by a single gunman. The King family was awarded $100 in damages. Jowers died in 2000.

Dexter King took on the role of publicizing his family's belief that Ray was innocent. Martin also believed that a conspiracy took his father's life. He still gets calls today from people who have information about the murder. He says the verdict in the civil suit helped him deal with his grief. "At some point you gotta release. And probably the last degree of releasing occurred once we found out the truth in the assassination. Once I had the information, then I could go forward with my life. I was in a holding pattern, wondering how it really happened."

The King children's quest to find their father's killer may have vindicated their suspicions. But their refusal to accept the conventional story about their father's murder hurt them in the public's eyes, Young says. "As long as they were content to just be the First Family of Black America, and hold onto the dream, there's no problem. When they started raising questions about this, they started getting negative articles all over the place. They started challenging their motives. . . . I think the entire family was persecuted because of that."

Finding out who killed King was not as crucial for the men in his inner circle, Young says. "It wasn't important for us to know who killed Martin Luther King. The important thing for us was to not let his movement die. And to get distracted by trying to punish a single person or even knowing who that person was took away from continuing the movement."

Yet no issue has hurt the King family publicly more than their demands for money for the use of their father's image or words. Many people believe that King's image and words belong to history. He can't be a symbol for the ages and a symbol for profit at the same time, the reasoning goes.

The criticism directed at the King family is partly based on comparisons. When King was alive, he made no effort to amass wealth. He didn't accept a salary as head of the SCLC. He gave away his Nobel Peace Prize money. Most of his speaking fees went to the SCLC.

But in recent years, the King family has aggressively moved to demand payment for the use of the civil rights leader's image. They sued the late Henry Hampton, who produced *Eyes on the Prize*, the award-winning television documentary on the civil rights movement, for using King's image. Hampton later settled. In 1993, the King family sued *USA Today* when it reprinted the "I Have a Dream" speech to mark the thirtieth anniversary of the March on Washington. That suit, too, was settled out of court. And in 1999, a potential sale of King's papers to the Library of Congress was derailed when the family insisted on retaining copyright control, and therefore future royalties, from their use. The King family had already agreed to sell the papers to the library for $20 million.

While preventing the commercial exploitation of Dr. King's image, his family has sold it themselves for several controversial commercial ads. In a Cingular telephone company ad, Martin Luther King Jr. shared time with Kermit the Frog and Homer Simpson. In another for Alcatel, a French telecommunications company, the civil rights leader delivers his historic "I Have a Dream" speech to an empty Washington, D.C., mall.

Some have called these attempts to harness the commercial poten-tial of Dr. King's image offensive. But Martin points out that when his father was alive, he copyrighted his works and sued to protect his image from being used for tacky commercial endeavors. "We're not trying to profit from the legacy, we're trying to protect it." If his family was just interested in money, Martin says, they would allow their father's image to be used a lot more than it is. "My father wore Fruit of the Looms but you're never going to see us use his image to sell underwear. It has to be tasteful."

Martin says there's a double standard applied to the King family. "My father gave away everything. He didn't worry about money. People expect us to be like him."

Young agrees that the criticism of the King family's attempt to pro-tect and profit from King's image is "totally unfair." "It's their right. You have to respect black people's intellectual property, too. Dexter learned about this through the music industry when these white producers were stealing all of these black folks' songs and not giving them royal-ties. They fought it."

Young says there are more sinister motives behind people's argu-ment that King's image belongs to posterity, not to the family. He referred to a confrontation between the National Park Service and the King family in 1994 over a proposal to build a museum in Atlanta ded-icated to King. The museum was eventually built despite objections, but the family wanted to build their own. "The Parks Department wanted to take Martin Luther King's image, and in their exhibition, they had the 'I Have a Dream' speech, but they didn't have anything about the Poor People's Campaign, nothing about the war in Vietnam. Even out in California, they tried to say that Martin's statement—'I want my chil-dren to be judged by the content of their character'—was anti-affirma-tive action."

Martin says the criticism of him and his family is also part of a larger plot; he believes powerful people have orchestrated the smearing of his name and his mission since he was born. It's why he doesn't take criticism personally. "You squash someone else so that people who are decision makers never take you seriously. Those who are at a certain level of power don't ever want to see it [the King name] become what it could. In theory, you should be able to mobilize all kinds of people around the name Martin Luther King. There's a concerted effort to keep us at a certain level so that we could never achieve those things that could make us successful."

As Martin presses on, though, he is aware that some of the limitations on his ambitions are self-imposed. "No matter what I do, I guess I'm driven, but I'm not driven to the point where I will go out. . . . I'll put it this way. Daddy used to say if a man hasn't found something worth dying for, he isn't fit to live. I'm not sure I got that."

But he still has the obligations of his name. He's no longer Little Marty. Yet late at night, when he returns to the home he shares with his mother, he's still closing the blinds and locking the door.

———— ✺ ————

On November 18, 2003, approximately eight months after we spoke, King resigned as head of the SCLC. He no longer lives with his mother.

Ilyasah Shabazz
Daughter of Malcolm X

THE WHISPERS BEGAN AS SOON AS STUDENTS at the State University of New Paltz in upstate New York spotted her. She was a lanky seventeen-year-old freshman with a ponytail, heading to her first day of college classes, but to the students who spotted her she was much more.

"There she goes!"

"Are you certain that's Malcolm X's daughter?"

"She sure doesn't look like it."

The word had already hit campus before she got there. Ilyasah (pronounced ee-lee-AH-sah) Shabazz, the daughter of El-Hajj Malik El-Shabazz—otherwise known as Malcolm X—had arrived. The news spread quickly among the black students. They not only welcomed her, but also moved her into the college's black dormitory and elected her as an officer in the Black Student Union.

The entire series of events stunned Ilyasah. But it was something she would have to grow accustomed to. Ilyasah's classmates expected a Black Muslim who would light up the campus with fiery speeches and regale them with tales of her legendary father, the most potent symbol of black separatism of the civil rights movement. What they got instead was a shy, middle-class woman who had grown up attending private schools with white students and listening to Madonna. She knew so little about her father she had to buy his autobiography to learn more.

"Today I understand that you don't go around and try to please people; you please God and that's it," Ilyasah says. "But back then, the expectations were overwhelming."

Those expectations don't seem overwhelming anymore. Now forty-one years old—she's the third of Malcolm X's six daughters—the stylish woman I meet in Atlanta is a lot different from the person I'd imagined.

Ilyasah's life has been filled with tragedy. Her father was shot to death in front of her eyes when she was two years old. Her sister, Qubi-

Malcolm X, in a contemplative mood, waits for a press
conference to begin on March 26, 1964.

lah, was arrested in 1995 for plotting to kill Nation of Islam leader Min-
ister Louis Farrakhan, the man she believed caused her father's death.
Then Ilyasah lost the emotional pillar of her life—her mother, Dr. Betty
Shabazz—in a house fire set by her troubled nephew.

Yet when Ilyasah shares her story with me, there is no hint of self-
pity, no sense of being haunted. She's cheerful, even playful, in person.
"I think that's because that's how my mother raised us. That's what
Islam is all about, submitting to God and to peace. Because when you
think about it, you're not the only person that suffers. Everyone lost
their parent. Everyone lost someone and everyone suffered. But if you

Ilyasah Shabazz and all of her sisters with their mother at a memorial for Malcolm X. Top row, left to right: Qubilah and Attallah. Bottom row, left to right: Malikah; Ilyasah; their mother, Betty Shabazz; Gamilah; and Malaak.

Reprinted with permission of Merrill A. Roberts Jr.

look at it like you're a victim, how do you accomplish anything in life? How do you give?"

What Ilyasah recently gave was her account of being Malcolm X's daughter—in a book titled *Growing Up X*. Before it came out in 2002, I talked to her by phone from her home in New York. She worried that her life would appear boring. "I just don't want it to suck," she said.

But the book's subsequent publication seems to have liberated her. She discovered an audience that empathized with her. She was featured in magazines and newspapers and was nominated for an NAACP image award. Shabazz had originally wanted to be a model or a songwriter; now, with the book, she's finally found the spotlight.

At a book signing in Atlanta, Ilyasah seems to revel in the attention. She enters Borders wearing sunglasses perched on top of her hair, a cream-colored suit, and black leather sandals. Long-limbed like her father (she's five-foot-ten), she displays a smile that seems to envelop her face—also just like her father's.

Some of the people in the crowd look at her in awe. Three young Black Muslim women in long flowing dresses and head wraps are too shy to even approach her. "I just wanted to see her," one says as she looks wide-eyed at Ilyasah from a distance.

Ilyasah, though, doesn't seem to want to be treated as a star. She keeps getting out of her seat to personally thank people for coming. "Let me give you a hug," she says, wrapping yet another well-wisher in an embrace. After one man haltingly asks if she can make her book out to

Betty Shabazz, Malcolm X's widow and Ilyasah's mother, with her grandson, "Little" Malcolm. Malcolm would later set the fire in Betty Shabazz's home that would claim her life.

Courtesy of Ilyasah Shabazz

Charles, she says, "I can make it out to Charles, I can make it out to Bill, whatever you want," before laughing.

Not too long ago, Ilyasah wasn't so comfortable talking about herself or her father in public. Her mother raised her and her five sisters in an integrated community in Mount Vernon, New York. Ilyasah describes a childhood that was middle class with a vengeance: ballet lessons, music lessons, private elite summer camps, and membership in Jack & Jill of America (a black volunteer organization for middle-class blacks).

Through her mother, she knew that her father was an important martyred civil rights leader, but that was about all she knew. Her mother also took Ilyasah and her sisters to the mosque every Sunday and hired a tutor to teach her children black history and Arabic. Yet overall, her upbringing was apolitical—no rallies, no participation in demonstrations, no insistence that she become like her father.

Her memories of him are fragmentary. "I remember certain pictures and I try to remember that time and I don't know if I'm remembering the time because it just went into my head or because of the stories she [her mother] shared and kept them going on so for long," Ilyasah says.

Though she was in the Audubon Ballroom in Harlem when her father was shot to death, she was only two years old at the time. "I have no memory of any of it," she wrote in *Growing Up X*. "From these experiences I carry only a dislike of endings, a lingering uneasiness with good-byes."

One widely reproduced photo shows her glassy-eyed father being wheeled out of the ballroom on a stretcher after he was mortally wounded. In her book, Ilyasah said she could never look at the photo "without half-covering my eyes. When I was young, that photograph was deeply disturbing and painful to me. Yet some part of me had to see it, to see his eyes, his mouth, his teeth, his chest, his arms, everything. I always wondered how he was feeling. Did it hurt? Was it painful? Was he scared?" As a little girl, she used to stay up at night eating oatmeal cookies with her father and watching the evening news. To this day, she has a cookie fetish and goes to sleep at night with the television on.

Ilyasah Shabazz at Camp Betsey Cox, a summer camp in upstate New York.

In her childhood home, her father's presence was strong even after his death. Photographs of him were spread throughout the house, his briefcase and suits still rested in her mother's closet, and their library contained books about him, particularly his autobiography.

And though Ilyasah can't remember her father, many others do. Their memories cause them to place their expectations on her. Those expectations really hit in college when people learned who she was before she arrived. Invited to speak at various political rallies, Ilyasah accepted, though she didn't feel she had anything to say. "They're expecting a Malcolm X to just come walking across the stage, really not even knowing who Malcolm X is," she tells me. "They're just expecting a lightning sermon and the answers to everything. And if you don't have it, it's a disappointment."

Ilyasah felt inadequate as an inspirational speaker. She was a young woman who grew up sheltered by her mom. She had no rage, no fount of wisdom to draw from—only her last name. But she continued to accept the invitations because she didn't want to dishonor her father's memory. "I didn't want to take away from what my father represented. And I felt if I didn't give the speech, it would take away from my father. I didn't have a choice."

Ilyasah started having more questions about her father. Who was he really? How did he think or feel? She sequestered herself in her dorm room to read *The Autobiography of Malcolm X*. She wept as she turned the pages. She even enrolled in a college course to learn more about her father.

I asked her how reading her father's autobiography for the first time affected her. She said the part that touched her most deeply was how the Nation of Islam had abandoned him at the end of his life. "I just remember being very emotional and him being so giving of himself. To be so giving and to be betrayed—no one there to help him, no one there to offer him any serious support after he just gave himself."

In his autobiography, Malcolm X predicted that the Nation of Islam would murder him for publicly revealing that its founder, Elijah Muhammad, had sired several children during extramarital affairs.

Courtesy of Ilyasah Shabazz

Ilyasah Shabazz, far right, with her oldest sister, Atallah, far left, and her sister, Malaak, in middle.

Even Muhammad's son, Warith Deen Muhammad, said that the Nation of Islam was responsible in part for Malcolm's death.

Her father's break with the Nation of Islam has apparently affected Ilyasah's family. Her oldest sister, Attallah, appeared on the television show *60 Minutes* for a public reconciliation with Minister Louis Farrakhan, now head of the Nation of the Islam. But another sister, Qubilah, was arrested in 1995 for conspiring in a plot to have Farrakhan killed in revenge for her father's murder. In a plea bargain, Qubilah agreed to receive psychological and alcohol-abuse treatment.

When I ask her if she is still angry with the Nation of Islam, Ilyasah pauses and collects her words. "Not angry. You can have friends who you think are your good friends and you could be working on this project with them and you know it would be great. Then when you have those who are envious because you're getting more attention, the project falls apart." Ilyasah then notes that her father had $600 in his bank account when he died and the Nation now "has its millions."

"I probably shouldn't even talk about the Nation of Islam," she says. "I don't really think about them often but when I do see programs and they start acknowledging individuals, I always wonder, when are they going to just acknowledge my father who really sacrificed his life and lived by their teachings?"

Ilyasah has never talked with Minister Farrakhan about her feelings, but when I ask her if she would one day make such a request, she says, "Absolutely."

Though she had always ached for her father, Ilyasah for many years had avoided visiting his grave. She finally made the trip after graduating from college. On a rainy day near dusk, she went to it and cried over it for a long time. Then she placed her barrette in the vase on the tombstone. "I thought about what life would have been like if I still had him, if my mother wouldn't have had to work as hard as she did," she says. "She could have just been a woman."

Ilyasah's admiration for her mother runs as deep as her respect for her father. She learned resiliency from her mother, who became a widow at twenty-eight and had to raise six children by herself—all while managing to earn a doctorate and become a college professor.

As Ilyasah grew older, her mother started to open up and tell her what her father meant to her as a woman and a wife. She could see more of the sadness behind her mother's strength. "Sometimes as she was drifting off to sleep or when she was really sad, she would talk to him," Ilyasah wrote in *Growing Up X*. "She would say, 'Malcolm, Malcolm, why did you have to go?'"

Then, in 1997, Betty Shabazz died when her grandson, Malcolm, Qubilah's son, set fire to her condominium in Yonkers, New York.

"Despite what happened to my mother, she wasn't a victim," Ilyasah says, who shuns any talk of a family curse.

Ilyasah refuses to let herself be a victim of grief. Like her mother, she worked her way through her losses. After graduating from college, she earned an MS in education and human resource development from Fordham University. Today, she is the public affairs director for the City of Yonkers.

As she becomes a more public figure, she runs into people who seem to feel that she isn't militant enough to be Malcolm's X's daughter. Some have even openly criticized her. One woman told Ilyasah that she never would have known that she was Malcolm X's daughter because her clothes were so Westernized. "And I'm like, what are you talking about?" Ilyasah tells me. "I'm thinking, my father isn't even alive. You don't know what we experienced. Who are you to determine what should have happened to my father's children after the fact?"

Over time Ilyasah has grown more comfortable with herself despite other people's expectations. "I realized that I didn't have to re-create the amazing lives of my mother or my father; all I had to do was be my own best self," she wrote in *Growing Up X*. "I came to understand that as long as I was a good person, as long as I lived by the values instilled in me by my parents and incorporated God's will into my life, I was just fine."

Some people even seem glad when they meet her and see that she doesn't fit their expectations. "It seems like they're mostly relieved," she tells me. "They really don't know what to expect. But when they see that I'm not intimidating, they're relieved."

Though she doesn't remember her father much, she knows about his love for her mother. Hearing stories about his devotion has shaped the way she has related to men. When she was a college freshman, she entered into a relationship with an NBA player—only to discover that he was unfaithful. She dumped him.

"I was like seventeen then. That hurt a lot," she says. "But it just didn't matter because I knew my father was genuine. That was my yardstick for a man. If this person wasn't genuine, if he didn't respect me and treat me how my father treated my mother, which was my template, well, this relationship was wrong."

The only time Ilyasah's cheerful persona changes to reticence is when I ask her about the men in her life. Ilyasah won't reveal the identity of the NBA player. Though she recently got married, she refuses to disclose her husband's name or talk about their relationship. The most she'll say about it is that sometimes she wonders if she will lose him, as she lost her father and mother. "I talked to him about that too, and he thought it was morbid," she said. "I told him it was reality."

The reality of losing her father hits her more now, she said. "Later on in life it hits you," she said. "It's like a post-grievement."

It's a grief that Ilyasah doesn't share with her sisters. She said she's never talked with them in any depth about their father's murder. There's an unspoken agreement among them not to delve into the subject.

Neither she nor her family appears interested in merchandising Malcolm X's image. Though she's written a book that clearly capitalizes on the public's interest in her father, she says she's not interested in brokering deals to profit from his image. She briefly led a successful fight to prevent her father's personal papers from being auctioned off. But she wasn't upset when Spike Lee started a profitable fad by marketing the X symbol on license plates, T-shirts, and hats. "We feel proud that there are people who are interested in holding our father in esteem. We didn't really look at the ones who were making money off of it."

Ilyasah is no longer the shy college freshman letting other people's expectations drag her along. Now she knows who her father was, but she also knows who she is. And despite the hardships that have come with her name, she remains grateful.

"There's never been one moment in my life where I wished I had different parents," she says. "It's a lot of pain. It's a lot of questions. There are so many different things. But I would never trade parents with anyone."

4

Children of the Segregationist Leaders

THE CIVIL RIGHTS MOVEMENT has often been described as one of the twentieth century's greatest dramas, with colorful characters, inspiring moments, and stirring images.

It also furnished us with a memorable cast of villains.

Defiant segregationists like former Alabama governor George Wallace were the dramatic foils of the movement—civil rights leaders played off of them to illustrate the cruelty of segregation. These politicians were considered politically moderate by the standards of their day. But history will forever brand them as the men who stood in the schoolhouse doors and unleashed state troopers on peaceful marchers.

These men were also fathers. In this chapter, I talk to the children of three prominent segregationists: Wallace; former Mississippi governor Ross Barnett Sr.; and the former mayor of Selma, Joe Smitherman.

They all say their fathers weren't cartoonlike villains devoid of remorse; instead they were complicated men bound by their upbringings and the political reality of their day.

Ross Barnett Jr. is the son of the man who ignited one of the worst riots in U.S. history when he blocked a black man's admission to the University of Mississippi. But his son says Barnett Sr. would have been run out of office if he had renounced segregation. "That was the plank on every Southern politician's platform of the day."

Their children may accept their parents' weaknesses, but history will judge them harshly, says Dr. Susan Glisson, director of race studies at the University of Mississippi and a friend of Ouida Barnett Atkins, Barnett Sr.'s daughter. Segregationist politicians who stirred mass opposition to the movement in order to get elected have blood on their hands. "They had a choice: to play to people's hope or their fear. They chose to play to people's fear."

How did this affect their children? Three of them share their stories.

—∞—

Peggy Wallace Kennedy
Daughter of George Wallace

PEGGY WALLACE KENNEDY WAS WALKING with her fourteen-year-old son, Burns, through a civil rights museum in Atlanta one summer day when they came upon a photograph that made both of them halt. Looming before them was the image of Peggy's defiant father, George Wallace.

Peggy watched her son stare silently at the photograph of the man he called "Pa Pa." It was placed alongside a series of brutal images from Alabama's history: Alabama state troopers beating marchers on the Edmund Pettus Bridge; portraits of civil rights activists murdered in Selma; the shattered bricks of the Sixteenth Street Baptist Church in Birmingham where four young black girls—all about Burns's age—were murdered.

Burns turned to his mother and asked, "Why didn't Pa Pa stop this?"

When you're the daughter of the man who was at onc time the most notorious segregationist in the South, you become accustomed to explaining your father to strangers. But how do you explain your father to your own son?

That's the challenge Peggy and her husband, Mark, face. Burns isn't sure he likes being George Wallace's grandson. He wants to know if it's true that Pa Pa did all those mean things to blacks. "He is just really embarrassed," Peggy says. "Every now and then he says, 'You know, if anybody at school says anything to me about Pa Pa, I'm just going to have to beat them up.' He's just having a hard time, wondering if Pa was a good person or a bad person."

Many people still have that problem today. Wallace is one of the most complex figures in the story of the civil rights movement. He once declared that segregation would last forever. His incendiary public speeches (one of his primary speechwriters was head of the Ku Klux Klan) encouraged whites to resist desegregation. His words also helped

Courtesy of AP/Wide World Photos

Governor George Wallace, forty-three years old and all jutting jaw, blocks the entrance to the University of Alabama as he turns back a federal officer attempting to enroll two black students at the university campus in Tuscaloosa, June 11, 1963. He stands with Alabama highway patrolmen.

ignite a chain of grisly events in Alabama that led to the murder and brutalization of black and white civil rights demonstrators.

When the federal government ordered Alabama's educational system to integrate, Wallace ordered schools in Birmingham to close and told a *New York Times* reporter that Alabama needed a "few first-class funerals" to stop integration. Martin Luther King Jr. once called Wallace "the most dangerous racist in America" and a man who had the "blood on his hands" for the four black girls murdered in the Sixteenth Street Baptist Church bombing. The bombing took place on September 15, 1963, when fifteen sticks of explosives detonated near the basement of a black Baptist church in downtown Birmingham that had become the center of civil rights protests. Robert Chambliss, a Ku Klux Klan member, was convicted of murder fourteen years later; Thomas Blanton, another Klansman, was convicted of murder in the same crime in 2001.

What Peggy remembers is the father she used to watch Friday-night boxing matches with; the man who always needed people around him to stave off his loneliness; the man who, though he styled himself a rugged defender of the Southern way of life, despised living in the country with its outhouses and rural isolation.

I meet Peggy in the downtown Montgomery office of her husband, Mark Kennedy, a former Alabama Supreme Court justice. A fifty-three-year-old homemaker who exudes a warm, almost maternal air of Southern hospitality, she talks easily about her father's legacy. She says her life revolves around her husband, her two sons—Leigh, twenty-four, and Burns—and her family vacations. Both she and her husband are Democrats, like her father: she voted for Bill Clinton and counts Jimmy Carter as one of her political heroes.

Despite her sunny disposition, Peggy cannot escape the ugly associations evoked by her last name. When meeting strangers in public, some have refused to shake her hand upon discovering the identity of her father. "There were lots of times where I wished it could have been Smith or Jones or something," she says.

Peggy was twelve when her father was first elected governor. Wallace, who had lost as a moderate when he had run for governor in 1958, won after dropping his support for integration. He electrified Southern whites with speeches that included his campaign slogan: "Segregation now! Segregation tomorrow! Segregation forever!"

Yet the racial maelstrom that Wallace helped touch off never seemed to intrude on her home life, Peggy says. In fact, her father never discussed politics at home with her mother, Lurleen, and Peggy's other siblings, Bobbi Jo, Janie Lee, and George Jr.

There was one exception. It was the first time that she connected her father to the civil rights movement. It happened in 1955, while her father was serving as a judge in the Third Judicial District of Alabama. Peggy was staying with her mother's parents in the country when her

Peggy Wallace Kennedy, daughter of George Wallace, at her Montgomery home in 2000.

father came by to visit one evening. Peggy, who was five at the time, was playing in the kitchen, near a wood-burning potbelly stove, when her father went to answer the phone. He then rushed back into the room looking worried. He said that a black woman had just refused to give up her seat on a bus in Montgomery. " 'Maybe there's going to be trouble,' " she recalls her father saying. " 'I've got to go back.' "

As she grew older, her father and her state became symbols of white hatred—his stand in the schoolhouse door at the University of Alabama to prevent the enrollment of black students; the Edmund Pettus Bridge march; and the escalating violence statewide. But none of it stuck with her, Peggy says. She was a teenager; she cared more about her friends than about politics. "I knew there were people who didn't care for him, but I was thirteen. Politics was never discussed at home. I think my mother sheltered us in a way."

But she couldn't avoid the impact of the movement at school. Her Montgomery high school was eventually integrated, admitting a handful of black students. Peggy says she wanted to introduce herself and befriend them, but she didn't because of her last name. "You couldn't go up to one of the black students—what do you say? They would have probably thought, 'Well, she's doing this for show or what else.' I wanted to but I couldn't."

Peggy says she never asked her father whether he truly believed in the segregationist politics he publicly espoused. "I never did," she says. "He was never really home. You grow up with that. When he did come home, the time was just not spent talking about that."

In 1972 Wallace ran for president. But while campaigning in Maryland, he was shot and partially paralyzed in an assassination attempt. Wallace, who had retained the cocky strut of the Golden Gloves boxer he used to be, was confined to a wheelchair.

Wallace continued to serve as governor of Alabama (he spent a total of twenty years in that post) but he changed with the times. He renounced his segregationist views. He started reading the Bible more.

During the first half of his life, Wallace sought power. But during the second, he sought forgiveness. The frail, wheelchair-bound man is the version of her father Peggy remembers best, not the defiant governor standing in the schoolhouse door. "He would call friends he hadn't talked to for a long time and say, 'If we got anything to straighten out, let's straighten it out now,'" she says.

That image of her father was so fixed that Peggy says she didn't comprehend the impact of her father's pre-1972 career until she was forty-eight, when she participated in a documentary on her father's life. The

2000 documentary, *Setting the Woods on Fire*, showed Wallace at his pugnacious best: delivering defiant segregationist speeches before cheering throngs, challenging hecklers to fights, and transforming himself into the archvillain of the civil rights movement.

Peggy cried after watching it. But they weren't tears of shame. She was mourning the loss of her father's vitality. "I saw him in a different light. What I had been seeing was a man lying in bed, sick all the time. And then he comes on TV. And there he is standing up. It was tough. He was so charismatic." She also understood the source of marital friction between her parents. "I could see why my mother was always worried about where he was," she says, laughing. "He was soooo handsome." The public footage of her father's "stand in the schoolhouse door," his defiant speeches defending segregation, didn't alarm her. She was impressed by her father's flair for political theater. "When he took a stand on segregation, he knew he had to do this. He said he would stand in the schoolhouse door and he did, knowing that they would still be admitted. But it was a wonderful way to get noticed. I didn't come to that realization until the documentary. Then it hit me. This was all for show. He was brilliant at bringing this on."

She says she was tickled to see footage of her father taking on hecklers in the documentary. He approached hecklers as he had his boxing foes. "He loved every minute of it. He egged them on. He would get up there with the best of them and duke it out."

When I asked her how she felt watching footage of her father giving fiery speeches about keeping whites and blacks segregated, Peggy became silent. "It was hard because I don't think that way," she says. "He could be hard."

Peggy says she knew during her childhood that her father had no animosity toward black people. "It wasn't that he hated blacks. He treated everybody . . . who cooked and cleaned for us at the Governor's Mansion like his own family. I saw it and swear to it. He would never mistreat one of them." Her father didn't just *respect* black people either, she says. "We loved them. Daddy loved them. That's just the way it was. We hugged and kissed. If you had disrespected anybody then Daddy brought the wrath of God down on you. That was not allowed, even though he took this staunch segregationist stance."

One of her father's closest relationships was with a black man, Eddie, who worked for him for twenty years. "He was my daddy's left hand and my daddy absolutely loved him. My dad would say, 'If I had to pick between you and Eddie,' and I'd say, 'I know, Dad, you'd pick Eddie.' They just loved each other and had great respect for each other."

Another part of her father that convinced her that he was far different from the unyielding segregationist he played in public was his sense of humor. When she married Mark Kennedy—no relation to the famous Massachusetts family of the same name—her father received a telegram from Senator Edward Kennedy, whose brother, President John F. Kennedy, had sent in the National Guard when Wallace made his infamous stand in the schoolhouse door. The senator's telegram read, "I'm so glad we finally got together."

"My dad got a big kick out of that," she says.

But her father also cherished the pugnacious side of his personality. One of his favorite photographs was a shot of him as a young Golden Gloves boxer. The photograph shows him driving his right hand into the bloodied face of a boxing opponent. "He loved that picture," she says. "It hung in his bedroom, where he could easily see it from his bed. He said it was the greatest punch he ever threw."

The last years of her father's life were spent battling grief. He never recovered from her mother's death in 1968 in the middle of her term as Alabama governor. Wallace had convinced his wife to run in his place because the Alabama constitution had barred him from running again. "For the first six months he lay on his sofa and sobbed," Peggy says. "I know when he died he knew that he was going to see her. Before he went, he kept saying, 'I'm so ready to go.'"

Wallace retired from politics because of ill health in 1986. During the last years of his life, black voters became some of his biggest supporters. At a tearful farewell press conference, Wallace reminisced about growing up in the South during the Depression, the attempt on

Courtesy of Peggy Wallace Kennedy

Peggy Wallace Kennedy at home in Montgomery, Alabama, today with her fourteen-year-old son, Burns, and her husband, Mark Kennedy.

his life, and what might have been. "I feel that I must say that I've climbed my last political mountain," he said. "But there are some personal hills I must climb."

In 1995 George Wallace attended a thirty-year anniversary reenactment of the Selma-to-Montgomery march—the same march he had tried to stop while he was governor. As the photographers surrounded him in his wheelchair, Wallace clasped the hand of Reverend Joseph Lowery, a colleague of King and then president of the Southern Christian Leadership Conference. "He came full circle," Peggy says. "When you're man enough to call people you had problems with and say you're sorry, that says something about you as a man."

When her father died in 1998 at the age of seventy-nine, he was no longer the symbol of white hatred. He was a symbol of change. His funeral drew thousands of people, white and black.

Today, Peggy is trying to get her son, Burns, to understand that part of his grandfather. Her son's questions became urgent after they toured the civil rights museum in Atlanta. He had never seen many of the photos before.

So what did she tell Burns when he asked about his grandfather's inability to stop the violence? At first she tried to explain that her father ran as a segregationist because that's what most of the people in Alabama wanted. Then she finally told him: "Well, you know, I really don't know. I don't know if Pa Pa could have stopped it. We never really will know."

Her husband, Mark Kennedy, says he's not going to hide the past from his son. (Their other son, Leigh, perhaps because he is older, has never had difficulty coming to terms with his grandfather's public image, both parents say.) "Provide the facts and allow your children to make their own decisions," he says. "But at the same time, give him reassurance that no matter what his grandfather did in this era, there were other good qualities."

Mark Kennedy acknowledges that some people still find it hard to believe that Wallace really changed his attitude toward black people. He believes Wallace was sincere because he kept asking for forgiveness even after he had left politics. "Did he change his view or did he change his politics? That's the question that will always kind of mystify all us— was it just politics? It doesn't mean that it excuses the situation but it will certainly always cause a lot of interesting debate."

Peggy says Burns is still coming to her with tough questions—and not just about her father. Once when Burns was talking to her about the difference between gay and straight people, Peggy interrupted him. "What famous person said it is not the color of your skin but the content of your character that matters?" she recalls asking him.

"I don't know," he said.

"Martin Luther King said that," she said. "It can also apply to being tolerant if a person is gay or straight."

Peggy leans back in her chair and laughs after telling me that story. "I thought it was kind of ironic," she says, "that I was quoting Martin Luther King."

Ouida Barnett Atkins
Daughter of Ross Barnett Sr.

WHEN OUIDA BARNETT ATKINS was four years old, her father tied her left hand behind her back to break her of the habit of being left-handed. He did it because he thought that his daughter would have a tougher time growing up left-handed. He told her nothing was made for left-handers and teachers didn't know how to teach them to write.

"They didn't know," Ouida (pronounced Wee-da) says of her father and her mother. "They thought they were being kind. But I would still pick up things left-handed. I still do."

Ouida's refusal to live according to her father's view of the world would become a lifelong habit. More than sixty years later, she's still breaking free from her paternal ties.

Ouida, seventy, is the only daughter of former Mississippi governor Ross Barnett Sr., a segregationist who sparked an armed insurrection against the federal government. Barnett, declaring that Mississippi would not "drink from the cup of genocide" by integrating, ignited a riot in 1962 when he blocked the admission of James Meredith, a black man, to the University of Mississippi.

At the time of the riot, Ouida supported her father's decision. Segregation was all she knew. She grew up in a world of debutante balls and black servants who pampered her so much that, as she once told me, "I never had to brush my own hair."

She says she was part of the South's silent majority. "We never protested. We never questioned anything. We went along and did what we were supposed to do. We just took it for granted that segregation was the way it was supposed to be."

But she eventually concluded that her father's views were tying her down. She repudiated his segregationist beliefs, even as old friends deserted her.

Courtesy of the Library of Congress

Governor Ross Barnett of Mississippi waving a rebel flag at a football game at Ole Miss, the University of Mississippi, on September, 29, 1962.

Today, Ouida teaches at an all-black inner-city public high school in one of the toughest sections of Jackson, Mississippi. When I called her to talk about why she broke her silence, she first began to talk about the event that defined her father's life: the "Ole Miss" riots.

The call came at six on a September morning, waking Ouida and her husband. A neighbor called to tell her that her father had made head-lines by blocking Meredith's admission to Ole Miss. Ouida called her father to confirm that it was indeed true.

She and her husband hopped in their car and drove to the governor's mansion in Jackson, Mississippi.

Her father's actions weren't shocking to anyone who followed his speeches. Ross Barnett Sr., while running for governor of Mississippi in 1960, had vowed to uphold segregation in Mississippi, no matter what the cost. A lawyer whose father had fought in the Confederate army, Barnett made no attempt to conceal his opinion of black people, frequently calling them "niggers" and making them the butt of jokes.

"The Negro is different because God made him different to punish him," he once declared. "His forehead slants back, his nose is different. His lips are different. And his color is sure different."

Barnett Sr.'s four-year term is forever linked with one man—James Meredith. On January 21, 1961, Meredith applied for admission to the University of Mississippi. His ordeal would last a year. The crisis culminated on September 30, 1962, when Barnett Sr. had himself appointed a university registrar and personally blocked Meredith's admission—though it had been sanctioned by a U.S. Supreme Court decision and ordered by President Kennedy.

It was one of the greatest challenges to the federal government's authority since the Civil War. President Kennedy dispatched 500 federal troops to the university, where they were attacked by a mob of 2,000 white people. Two people died and 188 were injured.

Ouida met her father in the governor's mansion after the riot had erupted. She walked into chaos. Phones were ringing constantly. People were coming and going to see her father. Segregationist groups from around the South were calling to give her father support.

Ouida personally handled many of the calls. "The majority of the calls, they wanted to blow up the bridges between Oxford and Memphis and anywhere so that federal troops couldn't come," she says. "We said, 'Please stay home.' I couldn't believe what I was hearing on the phone."

Nor could she believe what was happening at Ole Miss. "I never thought any violence would happen at all," she says. "My father didn't either. He didn't dream that he would have a riot."

When the riot erupted, Ouida says her father muttered, "Somebody has double-crossed me." He picked up the phone to call President Kennedy and Robert Kennedy, the U.S. attorney general, but discovered he couldn't. "He was so upset, his hands were shaking," she says. "I had to call the White House for him."

Even after all the violence erupted and lives were lost, Ouida says she supported her father's segregationist position. "At the time, I did," she says. "I grew up that way. We thought it would wreck the schools if they were integrated."

It would take more than a riot to change Ouida's views—she would have to go through a personal crisis of her own.

Ouida was born in Jackson, Mississippi, on September 4, 1933. Though her world was segregated, she grew up with black playmates. Her father owned several sharecropper's farms and whenever he visited them, he would take Ouida. She recalls jumping in haylofts with black kids and going into their homes to look at their new kittens.

She was in third grade when she received her first glimpse of the racial storms that would engulf her father. She heard her father talking with her mother about the Supreme Court's impending *Brown vs. Board of Education* decision. "Daddy was saying he was afraid the Supreme Court would declare integration," she says. "And my mama said, 'What will we do if those children come to school with us?' They thought I was asleep, and I jumped up and said, 'I'd love to go to school with them. It'd be fun.'"

Her father dismissed her, saying she didn't know what she was talking about. The brief exchange pointed to the complexities of segregation. Despite the brutal enforcement of racial separation, genuine affection sprouted between whites and blacks. Blacks and whites lived closer to one another in the South than they did in the North, which was considered to be more tolerant.

Ouida's voice warms when she talks about her family's house servant, Essie. Once, when her family took Essie to the Mississippi Bar Convention, the hotel manager told them that Essie couldn't eat with them in the dining room. "And so we all moved to the kitchen to eat rather than have Essie eat alone," Ouida says.

Still, tinged with genuine affection though those relationships might be, Ouida says she did not regard blacks as equals. "I was taught when I was young that they were not as smart as we were. I was not taught to hate people. I was taught that I was on a different level than other people."

Ouida Barnett Atkins with her father, Ross Barnett Sr., at her debutante ball. Atkins says that in her youth she had misgivings about segregation but kept them to herself.

Ouida says she never bothered to question why Essie had to eat in a separate dining room or why it was considered bad to attend school with black kids. Occasionally, she wonders today what would have happened if she had openly questioned segregation. "But I don't think it would have done any good," she told me. "I just took for granted that maybe I didn't know what was going on. I just thought they know better than I do because they're older than I am."

Ouida's views would eventually start breaking free from her prejudices. But first she had to break free from a bad marriage.

When she was twenty-three, she'd married Aylmer Buford Atkins Jr., a lawyer seventeen years her senior. They had five children and lived in the small town of Homer, Louisiana.

Ross Atkins, Ouida's son, says his father drank and was domineering. He was angry at the onset of the civil rights movement—so angry that he helped create an all-white private academy for parents who didn't want to send their children to school with black students. One of Ouida's first teaching jobs was there. Ross says his father warned his children to stay away from the neighborhood high school. "He told me the high school was off limits because blacks were up there. I was shipped off to the academy."

Ouida's marriage eventually collapsed. She separated from her husband, who died in 1976. She was now raising five kids alone. She could have felt overwhelmed. Instead she lived as if she had just been liberated.

She began to indulge her passion for travel, taking off to Italy, Europe, and Russia. Then she indulged her passion for learning; she earned a master's in ancient world history.

Ross Atkins, who today is a Washington, D.C., lobbyist who helps U.S. businesses find contacts in Cuba, says his mother could not sit still for long. "It was not uncommon for her to just get up and go. Even with five kids at home. But we always had babysitters."

And there was plenty of company when their mother was home. Ross says Ouida sought out new people as avidly as she sought new countries. "She had them all. She had a lot of gay friends. She had rich people, black people, white people, artists, musicians, coaches, and jocks. It was definitely good for us kids, good to not just be influenced by angry white men."

As Ouida's circle of friends expanded, her segregationist beliefs began to crumble. The person who inspired this change was, ironically, her father. He taught her to love being around different people. "My father had so many different friends," she says. "Most politicians do

Ross Barnett Jr. in his Jackson, Mississippi, law office today. Barnett Jr. took over his father's practice, and has little patience for people who accuse his father of being a racist.

because they want the votes. He was always telling jokes and having fun. He was fun to be around."

Her exposure to different cultures began to change Ouida as well. Her presumed superiority in not only being white but a U.S. citizen began to erode. "When I was younger, I didn't understand why everybody didn't want to be like Americans," she says. "It [travel] changes your whole way of thinking about people. Once you start knowing about what they think, how they live, it changes your views of them."

Ouida's reexamination of her faith also inspired her to question her segregationist beliefs. She had become a devout Presbyterian, but gradually began to wonder about the incongruity of her church sending missionaries to Africa while refusing to serve blacks in their own hometown. "It's hard to reconcile living in segregation and yet sending missionaries to Africa," she says.

Atkins Jr. says he could see his mother virtually reinvent herself as she sorted through all these questions. "You could always see she was out there searching for something new and different in her life."

Ouida found something different at Lanier High School. In 1992, when her last child became an adult, she moved back to Jackson. She began subbing for a friend in the public schools. One day, she was offered a job at Lanier. She took it.

Lanier, which has close to an all-black student body, is located in one of the poorest neighborhoods in Jackson. The area is so tough that some of Ouida's friends are afraid to visit her at her job. "It's like a Third World country to them," she says. "It's something they don't know anything about."

Her son says Ouida initially worried about taking the job because of the negative view many black people had of her father. That fear didn't leave even after she took the job. "She would wonder if they really knew and if they did, would they resent her," he says. "But it turns out most of them didn't know."

That changed in 1999 when a newspaper reporter wrote a story about Ouida's new career. The reporter pointed out that she was teaching at the same school as Bob Moses, a Mississippi civil rights legend.

Ouida says she had seen Moses around for years (she taught on the second floor, he on the first) but didn't know who he was. The two took a picture together for the article and exchanged pleasantries. But neither had much to say to the other.

Only later, Ouida says, did she comprehend the irony of the meeting with Moses. "Then it came back to me who I was teaching with and that Daddy had called him an outside agitator," she says, laughing. "He called Daddy his enemy."

In the article, the reporter suggested that Ouida took the job because she was "liberating herself from the stifling psychological confines that being a white Mississippian long imposed upon its ruling race."

Ouida dismisses that analysis. She feels no heavy burden of guilt. She took the job for another reason. "It keeps people young to have something to do," she says.

Two worlds collide. Ouida Barnett Atkins, right, stands
with civil rights legend Bob Moses, the man whose
activism in Mississippi aroused her father's wrath. In a
twist of fate, both now teach at Lanier High School in
Jackson, Mississippi.

When I asked Ouida's son if he thought his mother was trying to
atone for her father's sin, he didn't accept that theory either. "She didn't
sit around and say, 'How can I liberate myself—let me go teach at all-
black Lanier,'" he says. "She's been a teacher all of her life."

The experience at Lanier has changed her, though. After the school's
teachers and students discovered who she was, they accepted her. She
calls some of them friends. Before Lanier she never had any close black

friends. The daily interaction with black people made her realize how the segregationist beliefs she grew up with could linger even after she had repudiated them. "I think interaction with other people changed me where I never had it before," she says. "When you're taught something growing up, you take it for granted that that's the truth. It's hard to get it out of your mind."

The 1999 article gave Ouida some notoriety. She attended a 2002 commemoration of the Ole Miss riots and several seminars on the civil rights movement throughout the South.

At one seminar at the University of Mississippi, Ouida met Susan Glisson, director of race studies at the University of Mississippi. Glisson introduced Ouida to some veterans of Student Nonviolent Coordinating Committee (SNCC), the civil rights activists who made Mississippi the base of their operations. She chuckled at the memory of seeing Ouida talk excitedly with former enemies of her father. "She has this wonderful sense of curiosity—she doesn't have all the answers," says Glisson, who now calls Ouida her friend. "And yet she's willing to explore and meet people who might have them."

But Ouida's evolution has cost her personally, Glisson says. She's lost friends. "She's made some difficult choices. She was seeing a gentlemen and this gentlemen gave her an ultimatum that she stop teaching at Lanier or stop seeing him. She does not see him."

Ouida's transformation may have shocked her friends, but so did that of her father's nemesis, James Meredith.

Meredith, now sixty-nine, also lives in Jackson. He says he's not only a friend of the Barnett family, he admires their father, Barnett Sr., the man who tried to prevent him from enrolling in Ole Miss. He claims that history books unfairly treat the governor as a rabid racist. They rarely mention the way he treated blacks during segregation while practicing personal-injury law. "He was less of a racist than ninety-nine percent of all whites in Mississippi," Meredith says. "He was the only fair lawyer in the state of Mississippi with blacks. He was the only one who would take black cases and definitely the only one who gave them the right amount of money."

Even while political events pitted him against Barnett Sr. in 1962, Meredith says the two continued to regard each other as friends. In fact, Meredith says he and Barnett Sr. could barely keep themselves from bursting out in laughter during one of their televised face-offs. That face-off, immortalized in documentaries, took place when Barnett Sr. personally tried to prevent Meredith from registering at Ole Miss. Barnett Sr. entered a room where Meredith was surrounded by a posse of white federal marshals and asked, "Which one of you is Meredith?"

Meredith says both he and Barnett Sr. knew they were playing "a game" before the eyes of the nation. He was trying to end segregation and Barnett Sr. was trying to prevent a violent white backlash by playing the segregationist heavy.

"The game was to effect change and keep the population from being terrorized," Meredith says. "One time Barnett called for all the sheriff's deputies to surround the governor's mansion so that they [federal marshals] wouldn't arrest him. He knew the federal marshals wouldn't arrest him. He was trying to control the deputies to prevent them going off by themselves. Most of his shenanigans were to protect black people."

Yet Meredith has no illusions about Barnett Sr.'s true political beliefs. He told me that he believed that Barnett wanted to preserve segregation and was a white supremacist. But that didn't bother him. "I don't know the first white that's not a white supremacist," he says. "I'd rather deal with a cracker being mean to me than one being nice to me and steadily implying he's better than me."

Ouida also says her father was far different from his public image. When she talks to people about him, she says people often try to get her to denounce him. But she refuses to call him a racist. "He helped so many black people," she says. "He was the lawyer for so many. I never thought of him as being a racist. He always referred to himself as a segregationist. I think of a racist as being mean, capable of doing bodily harm. I don't think of him being that way at all."

Ouida's brother, Ross Barnett Jr., agrees with her. Barnett Jr., married forty-six years and the father of five children, lives in Jackson, where he runs his father's former law practice. Many of his clients, like those of his father, are black. "If you spent five minutes with him, you would like him," he says. "He loved to tell funny stories and give money to people in need."

During the Ole Miss riot, Barnett Jr. was a second lieutenant in the Mississippi National Guard. When President Kennedy federalized the National Guard, he had to march against his father's orders. Now sixty-eight, he says his father felt so comfortable with blacks that he left money in his will to two black friends, his quail-hunting companion and a massage therapist.

But Barnett Sr. apparently didn't leave his segregationist views behind. When he died in 1987, he still refused to apologize for his past. "I didn't make any mistakes," he told a reporter. "I don't think of a thing I'd have done different."

Barnett Jr. says it's unfair that his father's actions at the University of Mississippi define his career. He still meets black people who shun him because of his family association. One black man, a journalist, refused to shake Barnett's hand when he learned who his father was. "There are racists in all races. It didn't bother me. I felt sorry for the man. He has a small viewpoint."

Ross Atkins Jr. says his grandfather was a product of his time. "My grandfather once told me, 'In the North, whites don't care how high blacks get, just don't get too close. We don't care how close you get, just don't get too high.'"

Ouida says her father also told her something that helped free her. She had to travel to Vietnam to understand that while her father tied her down with his segregationist beliefs, he also gave her the tools to break free from them. She asked a Vietnamese guide if his people still hated America because of the war. The man told her that the legendary Vietnamese leader, Ho Chi Minh, taught his people that if they were going to be free and independent, they must forget about the pain of the past and focus on the future. "I thought those were wonderful words," she says. "My family taught us to not look back but to look to the future. That's what I do. That's what we all have to do."

Stephen Smitherman
Son of Joe Smitherman

STEPHEN SMITHERMAN DOESN'T LIKE "WHINERS," "country-clubbers," "hillbillies," and black civil rights leaders who specialize in "screaming and hollering." But he reserves most of his scorn for the black leaders who are now running Selma in place of his father, Joe Smitherman, a former segregationist and the town's last white mayor. "They're worse than the Bull Connors, the Jim Clarks," Stephen says of Selma's new black leaders. "These bozos are running it like it's the Wild West down here."

When I drove to Selma, Alabama, to meet Stephen, I passed a billboard just outside the town that read, "History Lives in Selma." The sign was designed to promote the civil rights heritage of the town. But that billboard took on added meaning after I spent an afternoon with Stephen. History not only lives in Selma; it refuses to die. The racial tensions that ignited one of the bloodiest campaigns in the civil rights movement are still there.

And so is Stephen, a man who is so eager to defend his father—the Selma mayor who opposed Martin Luther King Jr.—that he's already talking before I can finish my first question.

When I talked to other children of segregationist leaders, there was always an undercurrent of tension. They seemed anxious to defend their parents and to explain why their attitudes about race were different. Not Stephen. There was nothing to atone for. No soul-searching needed. No apologies necessary.

Barely fifteen minutes into our conversation in his downtown office, the fifty-two-year-old real estate developer tells me that he once called a black woman a nigger while arguing with her, but that he wasn't being racist; he tells me he thinks Selma's most powerful black politician is too dumb to have actually graduated from Harvard; and he assures me that blacks weren't really treated *that* badly during slavery.

The man saying all this doesn't look like an angry backwoods racist. He wears khaki pants, a preppy button-down shirt, and loafers. He's jovial, funny, and brutally honest—even about some of his own personal problems.

But when he talks for any length of time about race, some invisible switch is flipped on. He has to say something provocative.

Take Stephen's riff on the true nature of slavery: "It was wrong, slavery—don't get me wrong," he says. "But basically, the slaves were treated very well back then. They were taught English when they were brought to this country. You didn't have the industrial age. You didn't have the equipment. You had to have somebody to pick the cotton. . . . It could have been a control issue. I don't know all that. But at the same time, if you owned a tractor, would you whip that tractor? Or hit it with a hammer? You wouldn't. It was looked at in a different way."

History lives in Selma.

The most infamous moments of Selma's civil rights history took place in 1965. The clubbing of marchers near the Edmund Pettus Bridge; the bludgeoning death of Reverend James Reeb; the ambush and murder of Viola Liuzzo by Klansmen—they all took place in or just outside of Selma that year.

Stephen was thirteen years old when Martin Luther King led civil rights demonstrators into Selma. The protest centered on securing the rights of blacks to vote. Stephen's father, who once called King "Martin Luther Coon," had been elected to maintain the status quo. He ran as a segregationist and engineered the arrests of black marchers demonstrating for the right to vote.

Joe Smitherman was a thirty-four-year-old former appliance salesman who became one of the symbols of white resistance. But his son says his father was actually looked down upon by Selma's white "country clubbers" because of his poor background. "Daddy grew up in the poorest part of Selma during the Depression. He was on his own by the time he was fourteen. Now you tell me that wasn't rough."

Stephen still remembers seeing his father meet King in downtown Selma to negotiate over marches. "He had very quality diction," he says of King. "He was very smooth-tongued. It gives you chills up your spine now to think of it. He cared. Everything he said was authentic. I saw that as a kid. Dad saw it. Dad is nobody's dummy."

Before King and his demonstrators arrived in 1965, Stephen says, Selma was peaceful. "There wasn't any anger, bitterness, or hatred among the average citizens. You had a group of ain't-nothing-but-trash rednecks. But Selma is unique. We're not hillbillies here. It's the second oldest city in the state of Alabama."

Most of Selma's white residents were shocked, then, when their town of 20,000 people became the tumultuous center of a major civil rights campaign, says Dianne, Stephen's sister, now a corporate lawyer in Birmingham. "There was a sense, whether we were taught this I don't know, that they were happy with their group and we were happy with ours. I did not see any—given my young age—any desperate attempts or an outcry from the black people that they were being treated unfairly."

When Alabama state troopers attacked civil rights marchers at the Edmund Pettus Bridge, white residents of Selma were terrified of black retribution, she says. Dianne recalls returning home one day after the march to see her elderly next-door neighbor standing in her family's yard with a shotgun. He was there to protect her family.

Another memory stays with her four decades later. She recalls seeing piles of telegrams stacked in her father's bedroom from around the county. Some supported him; others criticized him.

The media portrayed her father as a racist, but she doesn't see her father that way. "The term *racist* is overused," she says. "Now it has come to mean hate toward a race. I think there's a little racism in everybody. There's racism in whites, blacks, Mexican-Americans. When racism is defined as hate toward a race because of their race then I can say, 'No, he's not.' I don't even believe he was ever a bigot. He was a segregationist."

I ask Dianne if it's possible to be a segregationist without being a bigot.

"I believe it is," she says. "It's this old separate-but-equal frame of mind. He has since realized that segregation was wrong and to that extent, he's willing to learn. Bigotry is an unwillingness to learn."

The Selma campaign was arguably the civil rights movement's greatest triumph. The dramatic Edmund Pettus Bridge march and the deaths of activists such as James Reeb awakened the conscience of the United States. That same year, Congress passed the Voting Rights Act, which opened political offices to a new generation of black leaders.

Stephen offers muted praise for the civil rights demonstrators who came to Selma in 1965. "They didn't know what they were getting into, but they actually cared. Some of them were blind to what the problems were, but they still cared. They had heart."

But when I ask him about some of the ugly events associated with Selma, Stephen is more direct. He says historians have misinterpreted what really happened in Selma in 1965.

Take the time his father called King "Martin Luther Coon." He says his father got King confused with one of his political advisors, Martin Coon. "He was going to a meeting with Martin Coon and they asked him an off-the-side question and he said, 'Martin Luther Coon.' That's what that came from. It had nothing to do with the word *coon*."

He also offers the inside story of the two most notorious murders of the Selma campaign, those of Viola Liuzzo and James Reeb, both of whom were white. He says Reverend Reeb may have been the victim of mistaken identity. He had heard civil rights marchers were buying clerical collars and impersonating priests in the hope that this would prevent them from getting attacked, he says. "Nobody knew who the real priests were. I ran into that in law enforcement. I had people who would go steal a car and wear a priest outfit."

Reclining in his office chair, Stephen offers another explanation for Reeb's murder. "The other story is the guy was dying of cancer anyway. You don't know what to believe. Somebody said he wanted to be a martyr."

When I ask about the cause of Viola Liuzzo's murder, his voice drops to a conspiratorial whisper. "I could send you to people with tales on that all day long," he says. ". . . Viola Liuzzo—out of respect for her children I shouldn't say this—but she was into a lot of sex down here. Who's going to leave four kids home months at a time and come down here? I wouldn't leave mine."

Stephen Smitherman, top right, poses with his family around the mid-1960s, when his father made national headlines in the Selma campaign. On the top left next to Stephen is his late brother, Tom. On the bottom row, from left to right, are his sister, Dianne, his late mother, Ouida, and his father, the former mayor of Selma, Joe Smitherman.

I ask Stephen, "If even the worst rumors about Liuzzo's reasons for coming to Selma were true, that wouldn't merit murdering her, would it?"

Stephen quickly shakes his head. "It was wrong what happened," he says. "But that [Liuzzo's murder] happened in Lowndes County [Alabama]—Lowndes County is a different bird altogether. These farmers, they'll kill you. We were different than the country people. These people will actually kill. It's the nature of the beast."

Class, not just race, figures prominently in Stephen's world. His conversation is filled with references to lower classes. For example, he blames the Edmund Pettus Bridge beatings on "redneck bastards" that infiltrated the sheriff's posse. He proudly points out that his mother, Ouida, came from a poor, Scottish family. "My mother walked five miles to school," he says. "Never complained about anything. That's the difference. All we got around here is whiners. The way I look at it: get out and work. Do something."

Of course Stephen has to deal with other people's presumptions. Most assume he's a bigot because of his father. He says they don't know that he's always gotten along with black people as well as all sorts of ethnic groups. "Most of my friends then and half of them now are black. My friends call me the *n*-word, the black friends of mine do. When I started to drink and act crazy . . . that's the way we do it. That's the way we live. We don't make a big bone out of it."

Even some whites outside of Selma don't want to deal with the town because of its racial history. "They're ass kissers," Stephen says. "That's the ones I deal with. They run from you. Say you from Selma—they don't want to touch a white from the Black Belt [the nickname for the area in Alabama that includes Selma]. The politicians run from us."

Some of Stephen's interpretations of the events in Selma—as well as his theory on the origins of the Civil War—may seem bizarre to outsiders, but they're common in certain circles in the South. Take Stephen's theories on why Reeb and Liuzzo were killed in Selma. They have been floating around Selma since the murders took place. Many historians now agree that the FBI originally planted the rumors about Liuzzo's drug use. But in some quarters, the stories have been repeated so often that they've come to be seen as the truth.

A window into that type of thinking comes from the conservative magazine *American Renaissance*. In 1995, it published a special issue that looked at Selma thirty years later, repeating many of the same opinions that Stephen voiced about the Selma demonstration. It also repeated some of the ugly rumors about Liuzzo, claiming that she had needle marks on her arms and "was not wearing panties when she was shot."

Another part of Selma that's perplexing to outsiders is the longevity of Stephen's father in office. Joe Smitherman managed to remain mayor for another thirty-six years, though the electorate went from nearly all white to sixty-five percent black. He apologized for his segregationist past and boasted that he appointed many blacks to run Selma's various town agencies.

Joe, now seventy-two, no longer talks to journalists, but his son offers his own clue as to why his father survived for so long—George Wallace. Stephen says his father survived because he renounced segregationist politics and embraced black voters. "That's the way he did his politics," Stephen says. "He learned from George Wallace."

Dianne Smitherman says of her father: "He learned early on how to work with all races. He learned to make that city work. He would appoint black department heads and he learned how to work with a black city council."

Yet Joe Smitherman's critics say he only adopted the guise of a changed man. According to many, he employed thuggish tactics and thievery to rule Selma behind the scenes.

Rose Sanders, a black attorney who led the coalition to defeat Joe Smitherman in 2000, says Smitherman dispatched police to arrest his political enemies on trumped up charges, stole absentee ballots, and offered voters money to vote for him.

Sanders was one of Joe Smitherman's chief nemeses. A lawyer and activist, she is the wife of Hank Sanders, a powerful state senator. She wields tremendous power in the city's black community, and she helped establish the National Voting Rights Museum and Institute in Selma. She also helped lead a takeover of the city's public high school to protest the treatment of black students.

Sanders says Joe Smitherman once tried to punch her in the face and called her a bitch when she stood up to him. "Fear or favor kept him in power for so long," she says. "The people he could not control with fear, he controlled with favors."

Joe Smitherman seems to dislike Rose Sanders just as much as she dislikes him. When asked by a reporter why he was running for office during his last campaign, he said, "I don't want Rose Sanders taking over the town."

While his father maintained his office in Selma, Stephen searched for his own niche. He attended the University of Alabama but dropped out just short of his degree. He left Selma in 1972 and worked as a

Stephen Smitherman today in Washington., D.C., with former Alabama senator Earl Goodwin. Smitherman, at right, is now a real estate developer in Selma.

salesman for Revlon Cosmetics before returning to Selma in 1976 to become a police officer.

That's when Stephen eventually created some controversy on his own. He called a black woman a nigger.

Stephen, who spent ten years on Selma's police force, blames the incident on alcoholism and the dissolution of his first marriage. In 1988, while making an undercover buy one night, he says, the woman hit him on the back of the head with a telephone when he walked around the store counter to call her boss when she refused to sell cigarettes to him. He admits he was drunk at the time.

"A black lady jumped me. Hit me," he says. "We had control words we use in law enforcement. I used the *n*-word on her."

Stephen left the police force a year later. Then, in 2000, he lost a powerful ally in his corner—his father. Joe Smitherman was defeated by James Perkins, Selma's first black mayor.

Stephen has little respect for the man who succeeded his father. He says Perkins wants the limelight more than he wants to help Selma change. Nor does he have much respect for Senator Hank Sanders, the most powerful black politician in Selma and a Harvard University graduate. Stephen says he doubts if Sanders is intelligent enough to actually have graduated from Harvard. "He could have but I don't see it," he says. "He would be smarter than I."

Stephen's blunt dismissals of Perkins and Sanders are characteristic of politics in Selma today. The city's leaders are constantly feuding.

In 1990 the National Guard was called out in Selma after protesting black students shut down their school over the firing of Selma's first black superintendent and what they claimed was the steering of black students to remedial classes. Many of the town's whites took their children out of the public high school after the protest.

Since then there have been other racially driven skirmishes: vandalism at the Voting Rights Museum, for example, and the march of supporters of the Confederate flag downtown. But the most explosive confrontation has taken place over a statue.

During his last year in office, Joe Smitherman approved the erection of a five-ton statue of Nathan Bedford Forrest, the founder of the Ku Klux Klan, in a predominately black neighborhood on city property. White citizens of Selma erected the statue five days after Perkins took office.

Many black citizens of Selma were outraged. Rose Sanders literally tried to topple the statue with a rope. The statue has since been moved to a cemetery.

Stephen says he didn't see what was wrong with the statue. He says Selma's current political problems are due to the emergence of a black political machine that has little to do with the civil rights workers that came to Selma in 1965. He says people like Rose and Hank Sanders are creating the disturbances. "They believe in violence. They believe in agitating people," Stephen says.

When I ask him to give me some specifics, he points to the fact that Rose Sanders once referred to youths she enlisted in the campaign to unseat his father from the mayor's office as "foot soldiers." "Why use foot soldiers when you're trying to have harmony? It sounds like war." He says the black community needs more black leaders like golfer Tiger Woods and secretary of state Colin Powell. "They're the best representatives the black community has right now," he says. "They have mild-mannered dispositions. . . . The Bible says the meek will inherit the earth. And that's what they seem to be going by."

Stephen is now searching for a candidate to back who can defeat Perkins and take on Rose and Hank Sanders. "I'm looking for someone like my dad to come up from the streets—white or black—it doesn't matter," he says.

Rose Sanders, when I contacted her, scoffed at his comments that she was employing violence to control Selma. "What most racists do is project their own racism and violence onto other people. Rather than acknowledge his own violence and racism he has chosen to demonize me."

She became angry when I told her about Stephen's wish that more black leaders adopt the mild-mannered demeanor of Colin Powell and Tiger Woods. "If we had mild-mannered black leaders, we would have never ended slavery," she says. "If we had just mild-mannered black people, we still wouldn't have the right to vote. If Smitherman had a choice, the South would still be segregated to this day and his daddy would still be in power."

When I shared Sanders's comments with Stephen, he shrugged them off. "Rose Sanders is a liar," he says. "I think she wants to be a martyr."

I asked him if he was worried that his comments might offend people. "What do I have to lose?" he replies.

Though some people may call him a racist, Stephen prefers another term. "I'm just a realist," he says. "I see things the way I see them."

5

Children of Black Power

BLACK ANGER DOESN'T CARRY THE SAME WEIGHT it used to. The images of black men pumping their fists in the latest rap video or scowling on the covers of hip-hop magazines are so pervasive that at this point they're cliché. America used to be terrified of black rage. Now we've made it a consumer item.

Yet there was a time when black rage was more than a posture. It injected another dimension into the civil rights movement. When Kwame Ture, once known as Stokely Carmichael, electrified a Mississippi crowd one night with his hoarse demand for "Black Power," he introduced a new rallying cry for the movement.

In retrospect, some of the black power rhetoric seems dated. What real chance, for example, did the Black Panther Party have of igniting an armed revolution in the United States? How many people really believed the Nation of Islam's teaching that whites were blue-eyed devils created by a mad scientist? Still, these groups were important for the psychological transformation they sparked in black people. The images of defiant Black Panthers sporting leather jackets and carrying shotguns or sharp-dressed Nation of Islam members marching with military precision awakened pride in a people who had been taught for centuries that they were subservient.

Three children of black militant leaders provide glimpses into the world behind black power. The son of Elijah Muhammad, the founder of the Nation of Islam, describes growing up in a murderous environment where his father was literally seen as God. The son of Kwame Ture describes the courage of a father who faced his death from cancer with the same courage he employed standing up to thuggish sheriffs in the South. And the daughter of Elaine Brown, former chairwoman of the Black Panthers, talks with self-lacerating honesty about living in a time when being young, black, and angry didn't mean you got a record deal. It meant that virtually all of your friends would be assassinated by the police.

Bokar Ture

Son of Kwame Ture (Stokely Carmichael)

SOME CALLED HIM STOKELY CARMICHAEL, the movement's bad boy who coined the term *Black Power*. Others knew him better as Kwame Ture, the uncompromising Black Nationalist who answered each telephone call with "Ready for the Revolution" until the very end.

By the time Kwame Ture died in 1998 of prostate cancer, he had changed his name, his politics, and his country. He had lived so many different lives that commentators who wrote about his legacy couldn't seem to agree on how to define him.

Kwame Ture's twenty-three-year-old son, Bokar, is having the same problem six years later. He's still trying to understand who his father was, what he represented to people at the height of Black Power—and what those answers will mean for his future.

Most Americans freeze-frame Kwame Ture as the angry black man behind the podium preaching armed revolution. But Bokar never knew that man. He never saw his father with a gun. He never knew he was such a revered civil rights leader. And he never knew he was a symbol of black hatred—his father had so many close white friends.

"He was just a father," says Bokar, now studying at the London School of Economics. "He wasn't, 'I did this' or 'I did that.' He never told me what he did really. He just told me what was good to do: 'Work for your people.'"

But his father's past could now determine Bokar's future. Since his father's death, Bokar has been approached by many of his father's colleagues who have questions for him: *Are you going to follow your father's path? Do you believe in the same ideas? Would you mind speaking at an event?*

For Bokar, a soft-spoken man who is just starting his adult life, these questions have left him confused. How can he explain his father's path to people? He's having enough trouble figuring out his own way. "I still don't know that much about my father's political views to see where I diverge from him," he says. "It's quite sad because when he passed away is when I began forming some of my ideas. I never really got to discuss those things with him."

When I speak with Bokar from his mother's home in Virginia, he reminds me of his father. There's the same faint French accent, the same love for Africa—he even punctuates his sentences with a hearty "of course," just as his father often did. Growing up in West Africa in Conakry, Guinea, Bokar learned to speak four languages: French, English, Susu, and Fulani.

"I have a tendency not to see myself as a West African but as a member of African people worldwide," Bokar says. "I feel comfortable on both sides of the Atlantic. It makes no difference whatsoever. I can be comfortable sitting with a Ghanaian or somebody from L.A. I can relate to them both."

Bokar's most vivid memories of his father have nothing to do with armed revolution. They revolve around his father's hospitality. His Guinean home was like the neighborhood recreation center; all types of people constantly came over.

Kwame Ture especially liked working with the neighborhood kids. Often he would stand on his balcony, which overlooked the ocean, waiting for them to visit. He would teach them math and reading; then he would take them to the beach to teach them how to swim. "I knew he was completely different from all the other fathers I saw growing up," he says. "People came over all the time, especially children, because my father was so tolerant. Everybody could come to my father's house and feel comfortable."

The lessons that his father taught him always revolved around one concept: revolution. For Bokar, the word meant working to change the lives of African people worldwide. "My father spoke about revolution all the time," Bokar says. "We would just be eating at the table and he'd say, 'You have to do this,' or 'Do that.' When he spoke, most of the time it had to do with revolution."

Kwame Ture in full-fight mode during the late 1960s, when he coined the term Black Power and joined the Black Panther Party. This image represents the side of his father that Bokar never knew about until after his father's death.

When his father wasn't talking about revolution, he was reading. "Oh my God—that's all he would do. I thought his job was reading. He read all the time—anything and everything. Books, newspapers just sat out on the table on the balcony. He just read and wrote."

But the revolution didn't pay well, and this caused tension between Bokar's parents. Many civil rights leaders went from being outsiders to being establishment insiders who made good money. Kwame Ture rejected that route. He thought capitalism was evil. He wanted to show solidarity with the world's poor people. "Money never stayed around my father," Bokar says. "He would give away homes, clothes, anything. I think he was a bit too nice."

Eric Ture Muhammad, a family friend, says Kwame Ture gave away all his speaking fees to the All African Revolutionary People's Party, an international political party he founded. He owned nothing but a car. "People would give him homes but he gave them away. He said they didn't belong to him. They belonged to the people."

Bokar's mother, Marlyatou Barry, a Guinean doctor who was married to Kwame Ture from 1980 to 1986, says Kwame's idealism got in the way of his being a family man. She says their marriage ended because he couldn't reconcile being a family man with the demands of being an activist. "I'm not against being an activist; I respect that," she says. "But I think life has to be balanced. His [Bokar's] father was a good person but I don't think he was meant to get married and have kids."

Though Kwame Ture called Africa his home, Africans didn't welcome him as he had expected, Bokar says. While his father rejected Western ideas—capitalism, its emphasis on individualism, even its style of dress—many West Africans gravitated to things of the West because they represented a better life. Even some of Marlyatou's relatives thought his father was crazy for his rejection of all things Western, including private property. "My father's attempt to claim his Africanness alienated him in Africa," Bokar says. "I think people have this idea of Africa being very African, culturally speaking. When you see my father, he's always dressing up in African clothing and rejecting all things belonging to Western culture. But many people in Africa are trying to grasp Western culture and are trying to leave their roots behind."

Growing up in Guinea, Bokar only knew fragments of his father's image in the civil rights movement. "Of course, I thought my father was the greatest person," he says. "But it was just him as a father figure, not a political figure. I didn't know how amazing he was as far as his political stance. I figure out more things about him daily."

Kwame Ture was one of the movement's most charismatic and controversial figures. In 1960, as Stokely Carmichael, he joined the Student Nonviolent Coordinating Committee (SNCC). His courage was evident from the beginning. In 1961, he joined several Freedom Riders who were assaulted by mobs as they traveled through the South to integrate travel. At one point, he was jailed for fifty days in a Mississippi prison. He saw his colleagues being beaten and murdered; he saw nonviolent protestors attacked with cattle prods.

He became known as the angry young man in the movement. He first accepted nonviolent protest as a tactic, but continually questioned its effectiveness. Then he dramatically broke from nonviolent philosophy with a rallying cry that split the movement in half.

Kwame Ture, holding his son, Bokar, while standing next to his second wife, Bokar's mother, Marlyatou Barry. Barry says her late husband was more suited for protest than parenthood.

In 1966, while addressing a crowd during a march in Greenwood, Mississippi, he first uttered the phrase, "Black Power." The words energized the crowd and symbolized a growing impatience among youth with the nonviolent tactics of Martin Luther King Jr. Whites accused him of black racism. The Black Power movement was born.

Taylor Branch says people who accused Kwame Ture of being a racist forget about his experiences in the South in the early 1960s. They forget how disciplined he had to be to restrain his anger when he saw so many black activists routinely brutalized. "Stokely Carmichael was nonviolent for six years in the Deep South," Branch says. "People don't have the slightest awareness. . . . Most of us wouldn't have lasted two weeks doing the same thing before we exploded. But he lasted six years."

The up-and-coming civil rights activist eventually joined the Black Panthers, but broke with them in 1969. He changed his name to Kwame Ture and left the United States for Guinea. He made his living by lecturing in the United States and Africa, but he would never recover the notoriety he'd achieved during his days in the movement.

Nor would he talk much about that notoriety with his son. Bokar says it wasn't until he'd moved permanently to the United States in 1992 to attend school that he learned the full scope of his father's reputation.

One of the first misconceptions about his father Bokar encountered was that he had hated white people. Bokar became aware of that belief when he attended an integrated high school in Arlington, Virginia,

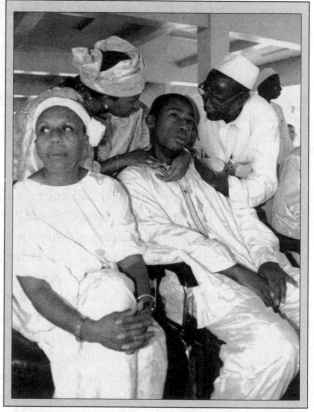

Courtesy of AP/Wide World Photos

Bokar Ture, then seventeen, son of Kwame Ture (also known as Stokely Carmichael), is comforted during his father's funeral in Conakry, Guinea, on Sunday, November 22, 1998.

where he lived with his mother. "It's funny because a lot more white students recognized who my father was than black students," he says. His father never hated any race. White visitors—along with just about every other ethnic group—visited his father in Guinea. "My father was probably the nicest person I've ever met and the warmest person I've ever met. Anybody could come and talk to him. He received everyone with a smile. There was a lot of warmth around my father. People always wanted to be around him."

Boladji Agueh, Bokar's high school friend, says students who read about Bokar's father expected him to be full of rage. "He's pretty open-minded," says Agueh, a native of Ghana. "Even though we've discussed certain things about colonialization, he's never made an open racial slur about white people, which is pretty common in black people. If he doesn't like someone for his ideas, that's what he's going to base his discussion on, not the person's race or religion."

But just as Bokar was starting to learn more about his father's past, his father became ill. In 1996, Kwame called Bokar in Virginia and told him that he had cancer. He sounded calm and determined during the conversation. "He spoke about it like a barrier that he had to get through," Bokar says.

Thereafter, Kwame Ture traveled periodically to the United States for treatment. Eric Muhammad, who became a virtual older brother to Bokar, recalled the night that Kwame Ture summoned his son to his bed when he thought he was going to die. He was physically fading in his Harlem apartment, and called them into his room to tell them that he wanted to die in Africa, but it looked like he wasn't going to make it. "As soon as he said that, he went into convulsions. He was fighting off losing consciousness by chanting rallying slogans: 'Africa will be free! You will not crush Africa! We remain ready for the revolution!'"

Kwame Ture then extracted a promise from Bokar. Muhammad is still moved by what Kwame Ture told his son: "You fight for Africa! Don't you ever forget Africa. Remember your place in Africa."

Bokar says, "I expected that from him. Of course, I would fight for Africa. That's what he instilled in me."

Kwame Ture rallied and survived. During his last days in the United States, his colleagues from the movement—white and black—helped support him financially and came to his side. In Washington, D.C., his movement comrades arranged a dinner to honor him. Actor Wesley Snipes and black politicians such as Eleanor Holmes and Marion Barry attended.

The mainstream press took note of his impending death. Most of the stories focused on his optimism. Though Marxism was on a worldwide retreat and Africa was mired in corrupt and brutal dictatorships, Kwame Ture still believed in his vision of a socialist revolution. "It is impossible for anyone seriously following or participating in the struggle not to understand that victory is inevitable," he told a *Washington Post* reporter seven months before he died.

Through all the tributes that came Kwame Ture's way, one theme remained constant—his tenacity. In the *Washington Post* article, Cleveland Sellers, a SNCC colleague and one of Kwame Ture's closest friends, said of him, "He actually was able to stay in, to go the whole way, no break in the struggle. He continued his whole life with that same intensity."

Kwame Ture was grateful for the tributes. He had been dismissed as a relic of the 1960s in the years that followed his move to West Africa, but he says he never became dejected. "What has humbled me is the outpouring of love," he said before attending the tribute in Washington, D.C. "Of course I knew it was there. I never stop repeating that once you sacrifice for the people, they will sacrifice for you."

Kwame Ture found the same level of devotion when he returned to Guinea for his last days. Muhammad says up to forty people a day lined up at his house to take care of him. People were sometimes *too* anxious to care for him. "They fought, brother. The Muslims wanted to claim him as a Muslim. The socialists wanted to claim him as a comrade who served the honor of the people. The family just wanted to embrace him and give him a sendoff."

Marlyatou Barry, Kwame Ture's second wife, says he never seemed devastated by his approaching death. He used to joke with her about a promise that he had made to her that he would not die unless she was present. "He was very positive, unbelievable," she says. "He was laughing up until the last two hours of his life. He saw my nieces who came to visit him and he was playing with them."

When I ask Bokar how his father faced his death, he pauses, then uses three words: "Like a soldier." At times he was virtually comatose, heavily medicated, barely moving. But one day, when Reverend Jesse Jackson came to visit him, his father roused himself to attention and welcomed Jackson into his room. "He carried it like a true political meeting," Bokar says. "He said, 'OK, Bokar, you sit there.' He was almost like a vegetable, but all of a sudden, Jesse Jackson walked in and he speaks to him. He went through this amazing transformation. And as soon as he [Jackson] leaves, he's back to being at rest."

On November 15, 1998, Bokar was in the hospital when he went downstairs to talk to someone. Someone rushed down and told him his father was dying. Bokar ran upstairs and opened the door to his father's room and watched the EKG line go flat. His father had died.

"After that I was told to wait outside," he says quietly.

Now people are telling Bokar that it's time for him to step to center stage.

Since Kwame Ture's death, Bokar has been on a mission to learn more about his father. He began reading his father's speeches, talking to his colleagues, and absorbing whatever he could. "People would tell me all these things, things I didn't know. People would study him as if he was Malcolm X. I always took that for granted because he was just my father. I figure out more things about him daily."

Now Bokar has to figure out his own future. He's being advised by people with different agendas. Some say he shouldn't attend school in England, but in Africa. Some say he should wear African dress, not Western clothes. And some, according to Muhammad, want him to be a revolutionary speaker like his father and speak at their events. People are pulling at him to see if they can keep that cash cow going.

Bokar himself has been tempted to cash in on his last name. Once, for example, when he ran into some difficulties raising money for graduate school, Muhammad asked him if he wanted to call in some favors

Courtesy of Bokar Ture

A pensive Bokar Ture stares into the camera today. The expectations for him to replace his father are building.

owed to his father in England. But Bokar said no. "Certain favors, I just don't want," he says. "Not for my education. I don't want to owe too many people things, especially people I don't necessarily agree with."

Bokar says he's even felt differing expectations from his mother. She wants him to stay in the United States and maybe run for political office one day. She doesn't want him to be poor like his father.

Yet he also remembers the promise he made to his father—fight for Africa. He says he's still trying to figure out what his father meant by that. Did he want him to live only in West Africa? Would his father think he had sold out by attending the London School of Economics? Would his father accept his explanation that he only went to school in England so he could learn the skills to help poor West African countries?

Bokar says he's leaning toward accepting a definition of working for Africa that doesn't entail living in Africa full time. "It's been a bit confusing. I have decided that the term *Africa*, I think, meant Africa as a whole, not just the continent. That's what it has come to mean to me."

He envisions a future where he may be as restless as his father. "I see myself traveling a lot and not having a permanent home," he says.

But there are other words that his father spoke that comfort him as he searches for a role. "I remember one time somebody asked my father if he wanted me to be a revolutionary like him," Bokar says. "He said, 'No, so long as he's doing something good for people.' My father always said give back. You don't have to be a revolutionary like him. You just have to understand your responsibility to give back."

Bokar says he's getting better at answering people who ask him when he's going to follow after his father. "The time isn't right," he says. "It's still not right. Even though my father was quite popular at twenty-one, I want to be prepared. I am stepping into the shadow of Kwame Ture. It's not too easy. I don't want to shame that legacy."

Muhammad doesn't think Bokar will do that. "His father laid a great foundation. The answers are already lying dormant in him."

Bokar already sounds confident that the foundation will hold. "Whatever I do, I have made a vow to myself that I'm going to help someone out there," he says. "The aim is not to be famous but to help someone else. I think I'm on the right path."

Ericka Abram
Daughter of Elaine Brown

ERICKA ABRAM SAYS SHE HAD A NORMAL CHILDHOOD. Her mother's friends were killed in police shootouts. Her family's phones were tapped by the FBI. She was constantly shadowed by a bodyguard, even when she ran to the ice cream truck.

Ericka, thirty-four, is the daughter of Elaine Brown, the only woman to lead the Black Panther Party. Brown took over in 1974 after its founder, Huey Newton, went into exile in Cuba. The group was about to implode. Many of its leaders had been jailed or assassinated and it was riddled with FBI informants.

But Ericka wasn't aware of all the dangers facing her mother. She grew up in a communal home in Oakland, California, where Panther members created a cocoon for their children. She attended a Panther-run school, read Mao Tse-tung's *Little Red Book*, and wore black berets. "A lot of people had this swashbuckling idea of the Panthers," Ericka says. "But when you're a child it all seemed normal."

But nothing seems normal when you're a Black Panther leader trying to raise a daughter in such a time. Elaine Brown was a woman who once pulled a snub-nosed .38-caliber revolver out of her purse to back off armed Panther men who resented taking orders from a woman.

Yet the same woman would become so frustrated at not being able to sew her daughter's torn dress that she would erupt in tears. "We didn't know how to be parents; we knew how to be revolutionaries," Elaine Brown says today. "I feel sorry for Ericka but I can't make myself over. She suffered in life because of me and I don't know how to deal with it."

Today, Ericka and her mother are learning to be mother and daughter. For many years, they lived more like comrades. Old habits persist, though. When I meet them at the Tubman African-American Museum

Ericka Abram, bottom row far right, at the Oakland Community School, the Black Panther-run school where she learned to live in the Panther collective.

in Macon, Georgia, to talk about their lives, both fall into the roles from their days in the Panthers.

On the surface, the occasion for their reunion is simple. Ericka, who has worked as a public relations director at the museum, is being given a going-away party before moving out of state with her husband, Malcolm X Abram. Her mother has been invited to attend.

But Elaine Brown quickly takes charge of the event. Now sixty, she still has a commanding presence that sucks the energy out of a room. Loud, brilliant, funny, and self-loathing—she can be all of that in a conversation. Brown leads her daughter's tribute as if it's a Panther meeting. She pulls people out of the crowd to pay tributes, moves the ceremony along like a traffic cop, and tells her daughter to cut an interview with a visitor short so she won't disregard her guests.

Meanwhile, Ericka sits upright in a chair next to her mom, arms folded on her lap like a little girl. She hardly says anything. When I ask her about her passivity, she says she's accustomed to her mother taking charge. "My mom has this rather aggressive personality and that's the reason I'm so quick to shrink from something. I grew up around so much confrontation."

Brown doesn't like it when her daughter shrinks back. When they lived together, Brown says she would actually walk out of the house when she realized that her daughter was becoming passive. "I would be angry. I would want her to stand up to me, but she was too intimidated."

Despite those tensions, both exude a palpable devotion to one another. In virtually every conversation I have with them, each is somehow paying tribute to the other. Both miss the Panthers' cocoon. For Ericka it was the one time in her life when her purpose was clearly defined and she was surrounded by people whose loyalty was unquestioned.

In the Black Panther Party, everything evolved around the collective. Individuality was discouraged. Serving others was the goal. The Panthers provided free health screenings and legal aid. Ericka worked in the party's program that provided free breakfast for children. She also worked alongside migrant workers.

It was a demanding childhood. Children were forbidden to play with toy guns. Duty to others was constantly stressed. If Ericka treated another child unfairly, she had to make amends by writing an essay on black heroes such as Jackie Robinson or explain why her actions were detrimental to her black comrades.

At times, the obligations were too much for Ericka. She craved simple childhood diversions. "Sometimes I didn't want the responsibility of being awake," Ericka says. "I just wanted to be like the other kids. I wanted to watch cartoons."

Ericka had two childhood heroes: Newton and her mom. They had a tumultuous relationship that Brown wrote about in vivid detail in her autobiography, A Taste of Power. It wasn't until she was about ten that Ericka found out Newton wasn't her father.

Elaine Brown sitting next to Black Panther Party cofounder, Huey Newton, during a press conference in the early 1970s. Brown and Newton were so close that, for years, Ericka Abram thought Newton was her father.

Newton died in 1989, murdered by a dealer in Oakland, California, during a dispute over drugs. He had led a troubled life: he was an addict, had been shot by the police, and had lived in exile. But the violence that many people associated with Newton had little to do with the impression he left on Ericka. What she remembers was his sense of humor, his charisma, his intellect. Newton was the soul of the Panthers, she says. "Huey was the sun and the rest of us orbited around him."

As a child, Ericka could see that Newton and her mother were close. However, "Huey said that marriage was ownership and that we were communists and that you shouldn't consider yourself owning people," she says.

The Black Panther Party, though, seemed to own her mother. She was so preoccupied with the Panthers that she didn't know when her daughter's teeth came in. Ericka walked for three weeks before her mom saw her take her first step. All of Brown's time seemed to be spent on keeping the party going.

The daily rituals, such as shopping, that typically bond a daughter to her mother didn't seem to exist with her mother, Ericka says. Her mother never did Ericka's hair or gave her a doll. In fact, Ericka could rarely be alone with her mom, who was almost always accompanied by a bodyguard.

"In the grand scheme of things, she thought that if she saves all black children, then she saves her daughter," Ericka says. "In my view, I wanted to be the only person that mattered."

But a girl expressing a yearning for her mother's attention didn't mesh with the Panthers' philosophy. They were trying to create a new model for raising kids. Parents weren't supposed to dote on one kid; they were supposed to see all black children as their children, Brown says. "She was a child but she was also the child of many other people in the party. If I had dropped dead, somebody else would take care. We didn't see ourselves as individuals."

But as Ericka grew older, the cocoon started to disintegrate. Ericka discovered that her father was Masai Hewitt, a Panther leader whom she first met when she was ten. She was disappointed: he had none of the charisma of Newton. "He loved Cuban music and books but not really people," Ericka says.

He loved weapons, too. He kept a hunting crossbow whose arrows were tipped with salt ("to dry out animals' arteries") in his living room. When he took his daughter fishing during an attempt at bonding, both became frustrated. "He was very upset with me because I didn't like smothering fish," Ericka says. "He thought I should have been a boy."

Hewitt was the minister of education for the Panthers, but she gleaned from comments made by his old friends that the education he dispensed wasn't confined to books. When Ericka would ask Hewitt's Panther buddies what he was like, they would either say nothing or give her cryptic responses such as: "If you saw Masai, that was your ass." When she asked if he killed anyone, they would hesitate and her mother would ask them to change the subject.

Courtesy of Ericka Abram

Elaine Brown and her daughter, Ericka, hug each other on
a beach. Elaine says her daughter gave her a reason to
live after the Black Panther Party came apart.

Ericka, though, rarely saw her father (he died of a heart attack when
she was eighteen) after the party disintegrated. At times, her mother
had to call Masai to remind him to call his daughter. "He would say that
he didn't know what to talk to me about," Ericka said.

The relationship between her parents mystified Ericka. They didn't
seem compatible. Only later did her mom explain it to her. They had
gotten together at a time when she didn't expect to live much longer
and many of the Panther women were encouraged to get pregnant. She
needed a man who could protect her. "She told me that this isn't a man
that I could live with but this is a man I could die with," Ericka says.

Ericka's mother had plenty of reasons to think that she was going to
die. Several Panther leaders had been ambushed and shot to death by
other black nationalist groups who resented their prominence.

The Black Panther Party originally had been formed by Newton and
Bobby Seale in 1966 to protect black communities from police brutality. But it evolved into a Marxist group that pressed for international
working-class unity and alliances with white revolutionary groups. By
1968, the Black Panther Party had more than 1,000 members and

chapters in twenty-five cities, including Los Angeles, New York, and Chicago. But its most dangerous enemy was the U.S. government.

In 1969, FBI director J. Edgar Hoover called the Panthers "the greatest threat to the internal security of our country." Only two years earlier, Hoover had created the COINTELPRO (counterintelligence program), which aimed to destroy black nationalist groups and their leaders. The FBI employed informers, played Panther leaders against one another, and orchestrated raids against members, in which some were simply executed by law enforcement officers.

Ericka's mother faced another enemy within her ranks: sexism. Newton personally picked her to lead the party, but when she took over in 1974 she knew there were armed members of the Panther party who didn't like a woman telling them what to do. Some, she knew, were willing to hurt her to prove their point. "A woman in the Black Power movement was considered, at best, irrelevant," Brown wrote in *A Taste of Power*. "If a black woman assumed a role of leadership, she was said to be eroding black manhood, to be hindering the progress of the black race."

Finally, in 1977, the pressure became too much for Brown. Most of her Panther friends had either been killed by rivals or assassinated by police. Newton, her main supporter, was exiled to Cuba. She left the Black Panther Party and moved to Los Angeles to protect herself and her daughter.

For the first time in Ericka's life, she was alone with her mother. There was no Black Panther Party to support them, no cocoon. Elaine Brown had to learn how to be a mother; Ericka had to learn how to be a daughter.

Both struggled in their new roles. Once, when Ericka asked her mom if she could have a party, Brown told her: "I will have to refer to a magazine to see how a children's party goes." Another time, when Ericka tore her dress, her mother painstakingly sewed the dress back together. Then she stood up and proudly showed it to Ericka. "I started laughing and she cried," Ericka said. "She'd say, 'I suck. I'm not a good mother.'"

Elaine Brown today at her home in Atlanta. Motherhood was more intimidating to her than martyrdom for the Black Panther Party.

At times, the two lived more as roommates than as a mother and a daughter. "We'd eat out four nights in a row and then we'd eat hot dogs and salad four nights in a row," Ericka says.

Brown says she was frightened about being a mother because she thought she would fail, as her own mother did. "My mother was someone I didn't like. I don't like her now and she's dead." She also just didn't know how to talk to an eight-year-old girl. "I was used to giving orders to men, men who were armed, at that."

Brown's long absences from her daughter during her Panther days began to trouble her. But her daughter didn't complain. Instead, Ericka says she grew to admire her mother for her dedication. Even when most of her mother's friends were murdered, she noticed, her mother didn't lose her fervor for the Black Panther Party.

"I know that I don't have the same courage my mom had," she says. "I'm extremely proud of her and sometimes I'm overwhelmed, because I don't know what would make someone that dedicated."

Her daughter may forgive her, but Brown has a harder time forgiving herself. Other civil rights activists may rationalize their failure as parents or simply refuse to talk about it. Brown, however, does not spare herself. "She's fiercely loyal to me," Brown says of her daughter. "I almost don't understand it in her. . . . She became second to the struggle and she always knew that."

Brown says her ability to be a good mother was also affected by the trauma of leaving the Panther party. The working-class revolution never came. The world remained the same, and she had to make a living to support her daughter. "We were both forced into a world I was bent on destroying," she says.

Brown had to learn how to nurture a young girl whose father was absent. But it was difficult because of her rage. "I was angry every day of the week after I left the Black Panther Party. I'm saying things like, 'Fuck this country. Let's blow it up.' What kind of character lessons are those for a child?"

After leaving the Panthers in 1977, the two had to adjust to a nomadic existence in Los Angeles, living in eleven different places because they couldn't afford the cost of staying in one place for too long. It was a strange period in Ericka's life. The woman who grew up in a communal home among black revolutionaries now attended a private French boarding school whose alumnae include Jodie Foster and Jamie Lee Curtis. At one point, she stayed in a Malibu home loaned to her mom by a Hollywood actress. "We're living in a beach house in Malibu and my mom is telling me that capitalism is wrong," she says.

But Elaine Brown shrewdly made use of the Hollywood contacts that the Black Panther Party had made. During its peak, the group epitomized the term *radical chic*. Brown had made contacts with all sorts of people in the entertainment business. She was also a songwriter with Motown Records. She used all of her resources to make sure her daughter went to the best schools and took art and ballet classes and overseas trips.

When her mother ran out of money to pay for her daughter's hobbies, she devised a novel way to save more money. "She just didn't pay rent," Ericka says.

Brown condemned capitalism as a Black Panther leader. Now she found herself furiously working all its angles to support her daughter. She did everything from taking a job as a paralegal to selling newspaper ads. Occasionally a company would make the mistake of mailing a credit card to their home—that became another resource.

As Ericka tells these stories, she chuckles at some of the situations. She calls this her "Down and Out in Beverly Hills" phase. Her mother knew just enough about the law that when they wanted to move, she would find something wrong with their apartment and confront the landlord with a violation. And off they went without having to pay rent.

Away from the cocoon, though, Ericka was changing. The girl who worked alongside migrant workers now hung out with her friends at a private Beverly Hills high school. She skateboarded and listened to David Bowie. The revolutionary child was growing up and becoming a Valley girl.

Her mom was horrified. She dispatched Ericka to Spelman College, a small, predominately black school in Atlanta, to "save" her. It was the first time that Ericka had spent a large amount of time around blacks who weren't in the Black Panther Party.

She experienced culture shock instead of homecoming. The students at her college told her she wasn't black enough because of her style of dress and taste in music. They were preoccupied with skin color—who was light and who was too dark. Ericka had never been exposed to color consciousness among blacks and later asked her mother why she didn't tell her it was such a big issue. "She told me that they thought that they were going to change all of that," Ericka says.

Many of her classmates were shocked to learn she was the daughter of a Black Panther leader. They couldn't reconcile their image of the Black Panthers with the Valley girl standing in front of them. "People expected me to wear a beret," she says. "Some would ask, 'Do you own a gun? Do you know how to break one down?' It made me feel like I should whip out a gun and start cleaning it."

Ericka then uncovered something unexpected within herself. She had stored up hostility against blacks. She saw herself surrounded in college by wannabe revolutionaries, wearing African garb and talking about revolution while they drove fancy cars paid for by their well-off parents. Aside from the clichés, few of them knew anything about her

Courtesy of the Atlanta Constitution

Ericka Abram at Harriet Tubman African-American Museum in Macon, Georgia, in 2000, where she worked as the museum's publicist.

mother or the Black Panther Party. Ericka knew the real revolutionaries, and she became angry. "They thought that if they changed their name or dressed a certain way, they've done something," she says. "And I'm like, 'My mom laid down her life and you don't even care.'"

Ericka took her anger to her mother. Was the sacrifice she and others made really worth it? "I asked my mother, 'How can you promise your life to people who don't care? They want a car. They're not thinking of socialism.'"

Ericka also discovered that she had unresolved feelings about her mother. Her mother's presence was so overwhelming that she felt like she couldn't carve out her own identity. When, for example, she would tell her mother that she wanted to be an actress, her mother would say that she should own the studio instead. And so it went whenever she mentioned a dream she had. Her choices were frivolous—they were never revolutionary enough.

Ericka began to question her self-worth. That doubt led, in part, to a fifteen-year struggle with cocaine, a drug she was introduced to not in the Panthers but while attending private school. "I thought, 'I'm never going to be my mother. I'm never going to have that passion,'" she says. "There's this huge hole. Drugs are the putty."

Over time, Ericka simply learned to keep her feelings inside around her mother. "I have a fear of her being disappointed in me," Ericka says. "I'd rather say nothing than upset her."

Today, both mother and daughter say they're just starting to talk about buried feelings. Ericka learned that her mother felt guilty not just because she didn't think she was a good mother. She also felt that she had failed her daughter because the Black Panther Party had disintegrated. "In her mind, she failed me because she didn't change the world for me," Ericka says.

That may sound naive, but Brown says Black Panther leaders really believed they would change the world. "We thought we were going to create something new or die trying," Brown says. "We didn't think we would leave our kids right back where we started."

When her revolutionary dreams failed, though, Brown found new hope with her daughter. She credits her daughter for literally keeping her alive. Brown dedicated her autobiography to her daughter: "For Ericka Suzanne Brown, Thank you for your gift of life."

"It was my life that she gave me," Brown says. "If it hadn't been for Ericka, I would have killed myself. I couldn't have stood staying in this country for another fucking day."

Despite the pain she experienced, Brown, who makes her living today as an author and a lecturer, says she misses her days in the Black Panthers. "It was invigorating. It made life important. It made it bigger than you. Even the notion of dying for something bigger than you was far more powerful than living out a life of quiet desperation. I was the happiest in my life when I was in the Black Panther Party."

Brown has nonetheless found a new happiness with her daughter. Both say their relationship is the best it's ever been. Brown also credits Ericka's husband, Malcolm, a journalist, with helping her daughter gain confidence in herself. "She needed this man in her life to give her separation from me," she says. "I'm such a dominant figure. She needed to find her own identity. But with Malcolm, she's free and can reinvent herself."

What that invention will be, though, is still uncertain for Ericka. She is now a freelance writer, but it's difficult for her to find a place in the post-Panther world because of her idealism. "I couldn't get a job in an advertising firm because I have so many principles," she says. "I'm not going to sell cigarettes and liquor to the black community. I'm not going to promote anything that's exploitative of women."

Unlike her mother, she doesn't believe in the revolution. She says racism is still too entrenched; black people in her generation are too preoccupied with making money; no one even remembers all those brilliant and dedicated Black Panther leaders she grew up with whose lives were snuffed out when they were young.

"I'm a pessimist," she says. "My mom is so optimistic. She thinks if people pay attention, people will change the world."

Only one thing ever gave Ericka that optimism too—life in the Panther bubble. But that bubble burst a long time ago. There are no more Huey Newtons, no more comrades, and the black berets have long been tossed away.

What she's left with is a question that she is still trying to answer. "If you've been told all your whole life that you were born for revolution," she says, "what do you do with your life when the revolution never comes?"

Warith Deen Muhammad
Son of Elijah Muhammad

HIS FATHER WAS THE MESSIANIC LEADER OF A GROUP that terrified White America. His best friend, Malcolm X, was murdered by his father's followers for challenging his father's authority. His own family threatened to murder him when he dared to break publicly with his father's teachings.

Imam Warith Deen Muhammad was a pivotal character in one of the most explosive periods of the civil rights movement. But most people know more about the titanic personalities that surrounded him than about the man himself. "His life is a mixture of the Bible and *The Godfather*," says Taylor Branch. "He's the most underrated American religious figure in the twentieth century."

Warith, who is known to his friends and family as Wallace, is the son of Elijah Muhammad, the Nation of Islam (NOI) leader who taught that whites were "blue-eyed devils." While most historians treat Warith as a footnote in the civil rights movement, he has a remarkable story of his own.

His story is made all the more intriguing by his physical appearance. A diminutive, chubby man who speaks in a soft lisp, Wallace disdains religious titles and entourages, and prefers to dress in a baseball cap and khaki pants. "I don't care for any attention to myself," he tells me in his crowded Chicago office. "I love the fact that I'm serving the community and people appreciate what I'm doing, but inside, I'm just a neighborhood fellow who likes to go to the movies and work in the garden."

Yet it was this unremarkable-looking man who did what even Malcolm X couldn't do: reform the Nation of Islam, disband its dreaded internal security apparatus, and become known around the world as the primary leader of America's Muslim community.

———— ≈≈≈ ————

It all began for Warith when his father met a mysterious stranger.

On July 4, 1930, a white man dressed in a maroon fez and pinstriped suit began selling silk door-to-door to poor black residents in Detroit. He called himself Master Wallace Fard, and told his listeners that he was an "Asiatic black man" who had come from Mecca to redeem black people in America.

Warith Deen Muhammad, then known as "The Chosen One," poses with his father, Elijah Muhammad, seated, in the early 1960s. A photo of the mysterious Nation of Islam founder, Wallace Fard, hangs on the wall behind them. Warith holds a copy of the Koran in his hand. He would break with his father after they disagreed over what the Koran represented.

Fard preached that black people were once a master race but their royalty had been stolen by an evil scientist who had created white people, a race of "human devils." One of Fard's listeners was Elijah Poole, a native of Sandersville, Georgia, who had migrated to Detroit in 1923 to escape poverty and racism. Poole became Fard's chief disciple.

Three years later, after amassing a following, Fard disappeared. But he left a tantalizing promise with Poole, whose wife, Clara, was pregnant with the couple's seventh child (they would have eight altogether). Fard told Poole that his seventh child would be a great Muslim leader who would "reawaken" black people.

Poole never forgot Fard's prophecy. When his son was born, he named him after Fard, giving him the itinerant preacher's first name, Wallace (the son would later change his name to Warith). Poole made other changes as well: his last name became Muhammad, and the name of the group that had flocked to Fard became the Nation of Islam (NOI).

Imam Darnell Karim, sixty-four, whose father was one of the first NOI members, says their message touched a powerful need in black people. The group emphasized family, education, and entrepreneurship. The group reached such people as drug addicts and prisoners who felt unwelcome in the black church.

But it also gave blacks a new way to see themselves, he says. "We were called coons, slaves, servants of white people, half-human. All of a sudden here comes this humble young man with a strange philosophy, telling African American people that you are God, that you made the earth, that white people came from you and that we had a great civilization. Man, that was powerful."

So was Fard's prophecy about Warith. It became part of the NOI's mythology. Warith became a golden child, a kid that older NOI members treated with deference. He lived up to his calling. He immersed himself in the study of the Koran, aided by tutors who were orthodox Muslims from the Middle East.

As a child, Warith feared his father more than he loved him. So did many others. Elijah Muhammad was a frail asthmatic with a fourth-grade education, but even hardened ex-convicts and tough street hustlers trembled in his presence.

Warith said he and his siblings believed their father had superhuman powers. "We would be afraid to think in extremes that would anger him," he said. "We would be afraid that he would hear our thoughts."

But Warith started to have doubts about his father's teachings. By the time he was a teenager, Warith had read the Koran and saw no mention of his father, Fard, or blue-eyed devils. Warith went to his father for an explanation, but his father simply told him that his way "is the way." End of discussion.

Warith's doubts persisted. He went public with some of his misgivings during his first sermon at an NOI mosque. He was only seventeen years old but he asked to speak because he was being groomed to succeed his father. "I told them, 'We talk about the devil too much. If we talk about the devil more than we talk about Allah, then we make the devil more than Allah,'" Warith recalls. "They loved it."

Others thought Warith had become a blasphemer. Muhammad taught his followers that he was the last of Allah's prophets and that Fard was Allah incarnate. Many believed him. Why shouldn't his son?

But Warith continued to question his father's teachings. "Because they said I was a special person, that freed me up to criticize, to question things," he says.

Warith's questions would become so serious that they would lead to a bloody schism in the NOI. The civil war was sparked by his friendship with the man who made the NOI a national symbol of black defiance, Malcolm X.

When Malcolm X joined the NOI in 1952, the group had an estimated 400 members. But Malcolm's incendiary speaking made the NOI national news. By the early 1960s, the group was enjoying unprecedented popularity. The NOI's searing condemnations of racism and its scowling, bow-tied members sparked uneasiness throughout white America.

After years of receiving death threats, living in poverty, and being shunned by former friends, Warith Deen Muhammad becomes the leader of the Nation of Islam on February 26, 1975, following the death of his father.

By this time, Warith was becoming uneasy about the NOI. He learned that NOI members were involved in drug dealing and prostitution. A few had used violence to quell questions about his father's authority. "Some Muslims were being beaten and a few of them were killed for dissenting," Warith says.

Both Warith and Malcolm X became disenchanted with the NOI at the same time that they stopped believing in its theology. And they both learned about a scandal that mocked the divine status that Muhammad Sr. claimed for himself. Muhammad, the "messenger of God," had fathered children out of wedlock with at least two of his secretaries.

The tension within the NOI was simmering due to other factors as well. In 1962 the FBI initiated a campaign to destroy the group. Its counterintelligence program used wire-tapping, informants, and planting rumors to force a war between Malcolm, Warith, and Muhammad Sr.

By 1964, the group was about to explode. Both Malcolm and Warith were viewed as outsiders in the NOI. Muhammad Sr., wary of Malcolm's popularity, publicly silenced his most popular minister. He then banished his son from the group because of his friendship with Malcolm and his opposition to his teachings.

Warith was now under siege from the FBI and the NOI. He received death threats at home from anonymous callers. He recognized the voice of one of the callers: it was his older brother, Elijah Muhammad Jr., warning him to stay away from Malcolm X. "You better stop what you're doing," his brother told him. "Do you know what will happen to you?"

"No, Junior, what will happen to me?" Warith asked. "I knew what would happen," he tells me, "but I just wanted to hear him say it."

His older brother (who vehemently denies today that he ever threatened his brother) repeated the warning and ended the conversation with that lingering threat. Warith was saddened but not surprised. "We were all raised to be prepared to sacrifice everything for the Honorable Elijah Muhammad and the Nation of Islam," he says.

Open war soon erupted between NOI members faithful to Malcolm and those who supported Elijah Muhammad. There were street brawls, ambushes, and murders. Malcolm reached out to Warith for public support, asking him to go to court to support the testimonies of the NOI secretaries, who were now pressing paternity suits against his father. "I'm hurt," Warith says. "I'm put in a very uncomfortable position. I don't want to say no to him. He's such a great person. We love him so much. He's Malcolm. But I have to say no to him because he is not a person I can now trust."

Warith says that he could no longer trust Malcolm because Malcolm had become "obsessed" with destroying his father. Malcolm was infuriated because he felt that the NOI used his charisma and speaking ability to make Elijah Muhammad famous.

But Warith thought his father could be persuaded to admit that the NOI's theology was wrong. He said his father wasn't a racist demagogue but a misguided leader who tried to build up black people's self-esteem through the teachings of black supremacy. "I saw my father as a man who needed help, not someone who needed to be condemned," Warith says.

Instead it was Malcolm who was condemned. The public exchange between Malcolm and the NOI became more hostile. Malcolm, who had recently converted to orthodox Islam, labeled Muhammad Sr. a fake. Muhammad called Malcolm a hypocrite.

On February 21, 1965, Malcolm X was assassinated in Harlem during a speaking event. Four NOI members were arrested. Warith's confidant and ally was dead—at the hands of his father, many people said.

"The Nation of Islam was the assassin of Malcolm X, that's for sure," Warith says. "But the influence behind it was in the intelligence departments, the FBI, and local police." Warith maintains that his father never ordered the murder. "He could be ruthless, but he was very careful. He was very careful not to put himself on the spot and actually give an order."

Six days after Malcolm's death, Warith returned to the NOI. At the group's annual convention in Chicago, he embraced his father onstage. Then he told the NOI members: "I judged my father when I should have let God do it."

Warith said he returned to the NOI to save the group. "I went back there in the interest of using my influence to keep them from going to more extremes."

Warith returned to save his life, says Karl Evanzz, author of *The Messenger*, a biography of the NOI leader. Evanzz, who studied FBI wiretaps of the NOI, said Muhammad Sr. was going to allow NOI hit squads to murder his son but backed off after Warith's mother warned him that she would go public with the NOI's scandals if Warith was harmed. "That's why he [Elijah Muhammad] backed off the idea of killing Wallace [Warith]," Evanzz says. "Had he not been a member of the royal family, they would have killed him."

Though he had returned, Warith would not abandon his criticism of his father's teaching. His defiance earned his father's wrath again. In 1966 Muhammad Sr. banished his son from the NOI.

Ngina Muhammad, Warith's daughter from a previous marriage (he's been married four times and has nine children), remembers that day. She was attending the NOI school when she was summoned over the school's intercom and removed from school. "Our relatives and friends disappeared and stopped calling," she says.

The chosen son then became just another blue-collar laborer on Chicago's Southside. He worked as a baker, welder, cab driver, and rug cleaner. He calls that exile one of the most liberating times in his life. "I was free. I felt free from the Nation of Islam."

Yet the threats continued. Callers phoned to declare that "Wallace [Warith] is a dead man." Someone mailed him a dead mouse. Warith told his daughter never to sit by a window in their home. Ngina Muhammad couldn't reconcile the malevolent image the anonymous callers had of her father with the man she saw at home. She said her father literally refused to kill a fly, preferring instead to shoo them outside. He wouldn't turn away a stray cat (they eventually had thirteen in the house) and he would constantly take street derelicts aside to encourage them. "I used to think he was so weird," she says, laughing.

At times, the tension punctured her father's surface calm. Once, when her father spoke at a mosque, a man stood in the back and began shouting threats at him. Guards carried him outside. When Ngina Muhammad went backstage afterward, she says, her father's hands were shaking as he tried to comfort her. "His voice was trembling as he spoke to us, and he had tears in his eyes."

Warith said he had just become tired of all the emphasis on race. "What is this big thing about race?" he said. "I'm not the man I am because my skin is brown or black."

By the late 1960s, the stage was set for Warith's return. The NOI had degenerated into a Muslim mafia. The group had acquired a bank, a Lear jet, five mansions, and a $100,000 bejeweled fez for its leader.

Some NOI members were even robbing banks, or so Taylor Branch claims.

Muhammad Sr., now in failing health, softened his stance toward his renegade son. In 1972, he told Warith that he could return to the NOI. By 1974, he had given him permission to teach Islam his way. Muhammad Sr. had grown to respect his son, Evanzz says. "Elijah Muhammad trusted him more than any of the other kids because he was the only one who would challenge his father."

Warith's reputation had spread throughout the NOI. Many members were impressed with his quiet courage, says John Ramadan, who joined the NOI in 1970. "He [Warith] was on a radio show one night and a brother told me, 'This is a bad dude. Listen to him. They put him out and every time he comes back, but boy, he gives them hell.'"

On February 26, 1975, Elijah Muhammad Sr. died of congestive heart failure. It was a staggering blow for some members. Many had literally believed that he would never die because he was divine. The next day, at the group's annual Savior's Day Convention, the group picked Warith to succeed his father.

The abrupt transition from heretic to heir was dizzying for Warith's family. His daughter, Ngina Muhammad, remembers NOI officials coming to their house at 3:33 A.M. to tell them of Elijah Muhammad's death and to immediately move them into his Chicago mansion.

The former welder now lived like a king. A staff of servants made up his and his family member's beds. Huge meals were prepared for them.

But Warith refused the royal treatment. "He offered to serve the waiters," Ngina says. Three weeks after he moved in, Warith moved out of the mansion. His plan didn't including ruling like a king. He wanted to take the NOI's kingdom apart. He would reform the NOI—a dangerous task.

"I couldn't attack the honorable Elijah Muhammad," Warith tells me. "That would be suicide. I would lose everything." So he began playing a dangerous chess game. The moves took place over a four-year period. First, he publicly praised his father's leadership but told NOI members that his father and the group's founder, Fard, were not divine. He told

Warith Deen Muhammad, with a painting of his friend
Malcolm X in the background, sits in his Chicago office
today. Muhammad and Malcolm were extremely close
but their friendship was strained by Malcolm's bitter
conflict with Muhammad's father.

them that whites were to be considered fully human and even welcome
in the NOI.

Then he took another dangerous step. He restored Malcolm X to a
place of honor, naming the group's New York mosque after him. Warith
also took on the NOI's security force, the Fruit of Islam. He dismantled
them after consulting in secret with the NOI's national staff.

Finally, he changed the language of the NOI. He erased anti-Amer-
ican slogans from the group's temples and replaced them with Arabic
symbols. The NOI, which he eventually renamed the Muslim American Society, was now following Sunni Islam, he declared.

Only ten years earlier, Malcolm X had been murdered for breaking
away from the NOI and challenging Elijah Muhammad's divinity.

Warith accomplished his reforms without shedding a drop of blood. Ramadan says the NOI accepted Warith's changes because they respected Warith's integrity. "A lot of brothers who were expelled went back to their old ways. When he was expelled, he couldn't even call his mother or go home, but he kept his morality and dignity. That gave us strength, knowing that no one was going to kill our spirit by telling us something about the Imam as they were able to tell us about some of the other officials."

Other NOI members accepted Warith's changes for simpler reasons, Evanzz says. "A lot of people just wanted to get away from the hate thing. They were tired and burned out."

In 1978, Warith broke NOI tradition again; he gave up his power. He resigned as the head of the NOI and placed the group's leadership in an elected council of six people serving as imams. He said the group's members would simply be known as Muslims.

Warith met with opposition. Some NOI loyalists warned that he was destroying the organization. And in 1978, Minister Louis Farrakhan broke away from Warith to form a revived version of the NOI. Warith didn't oppose Farrakhan. In fact, he asked his followers to forgo any criticism of the minister.

Warith may not have had charisma as a leader, but he had character, his followers said. Karim, Warith's childhood friend, says even Warith's enemies knew he wasn't interested in the selfish pursuit of power. "Even though you might find violent people, you might find jealous people, we all respect innocence. You will be surprised at the protection it will give you."

———— ✺ ————

Warith doesn't need that protection today. He's become a Muslim statesman, a man who moves easily between the worlds of Muslims in Mecca and in Chicago. He has spoken in countries such as Saudi Arabia, Malaysia, and Bangladesh. He has also met with Pope John Paul II and former president Bill Clinton. He was the first Muslim to open the U.S. Senate with a prayer.

Warith's grasp of Islam is so respected that the World Mission Council of Imam Administrators designated Warith as the Imam responsible for clearing all Muslim Americans who want to undertake the *hajj* to Mecca. (The *hajj* is a sacred journey to the Saudi Arabian city that all Muslims are required to make once in their lifetime.)

At seventy years old, Warith says he's developed a new perspective on his past. When his father helped create the NOI, he planted the seeds for African Americans to eventually embrace true Islam. His father taught them self-reliance and pride. "He preached separation of the races, but he was not racist in that ugly sense. He hated the evils of white people. He was not a racist. He was a nation builder."

And he has a new appreciation for how much he has survived. "I was aware that I could have lost my life," he says of his early days. "But I had faith that if I just remained honest and sincere and did not hurt anybody, I would do that. But there were times when I suffered pain in my heart and fear. But the fear of God is greater. So I could live with that fear."

6

Children of the Martyrs

THE CIVIL RIGHTS MOVEMENT is typically described as a mass movement: mass meetings; masses of demonstrators converging on places such as Selma; mass marches.

But here's another image from the movement, one that people tend to forget.

A bullet-pocked 1963 Oldsmobile sits alone in a desolate country field. Dead pine trees surround the car. The driver's window is shattered and the seat is covered with blood.

This is the car that Viola Liuzzo was driving the night she was killed outside of Selma in 1965. The Detroit housewife died alone in a field. The picture of her, widely distributed by the media afterward, showed a striking, luminous young woman with wavy blonde hair staring into the camera with a faint melancholy smile. She left behind a husband and five kids.

Liuzzo's death became a media sensation. Scores of ordinary civil rights activists died anonymously during the movement. But there were a handful whose deaths for some reason grabbed the public's attention, becoming symbols that people still remember today. These were the martyrs of the movement.

Forty years later, martyrs such as Liuzzo are figures in history books or faces on civil rights memorials. But little is said about their children. How were they able to move on? The loss of a parent is tragic enough. Yet the pain is deepened when the loss is replayed on the evening news and the child is too young to understand why the parent died.

Here the children—and one younger brother—of three of the movement's martyrs talk about life with and after their parents' murders. They say the shockwaves rumbled through their lives long after the mass marches ended. Some have never recovered.

Penny Liuzzo Herrington
Daughter of Viola Liuzzo

On March 26, 1965, Penny Liuzzo was watching the Donna Reed Show at her home in Detroit when a wave of nausea suddenly swept over her. In an instant, she knew what had happened. "Oh my God," she thought as she stood up and walked out of the room. "My mom's dead."

When Penny's mother, Viola Liuzzo, had called home earlier to tell her family that she was going to Selma, Penny had been engulfed by a sense of dread. She tried to talk her mother out of going. "I'm never going to see you again, Mom. I know it. I just feel it. Please let me go in your place. I'll go."

Liuzzo laughed off her daughter's fears. She had been determined to help marchers in Selma after watching newsreel footage of civil rights marchers being beaten there. She had cried after the newscast ended. "I'm tired of sitting here watching people get beat up," she told her family before driving off to Selma.

The call came at midnight. After experiencing her bout of nausea, Penny had gone to bed but could not sleep. She heard her father answer the phone. "Penny, your mother's dead! Your mother's dead," he wailed.

Then something happened that Penny still cannot explain forty years later. Her six-year-old sister, Sally, walked into the bedroom and said, "No, Mama's not dead. I just saw her walking in the hall."

The murder of Viola Liuzzo was one of the most shocking moments in the civil rights movement. On a winding, isolated road outside Selma, Liuzzo was ambushed and shot to death by a car full of Ku Klux Klansmen.

She was murdered while giving a ride to a nineteen-year-old black man, Leroy Moton, one of many civil rights marchers she drove around

Viola Liuzzo in her twenties, during
the 1940s.

Selma. Liuzzo had joined the movement's car pool system soon after
arriving in the small Alabama town.

Liuzzo's murder became international news. Her photo became a
fixture in history books. Her name has been inscribed on civil rights
memorials throughout the United States.

But people had far less sympathy for Liuzzo when she was murdered. Hate mail flooded her Detroit home, accusing her of being a
deranged communist. Crosses were burned in front of her home. Her
husband, Anthony Liuzzo Sr., had to hire armed guards to protect his
family.

A *Ladies' Home Journal* magazine survey taken right after Liuzzo's
death asked its readers what kind of woman would leave her family for
a civil rights demonstration. The magazine suggested that she had
brought death on herself by leaving home—and fifty-five percent of its
readers agreed.

"It was horrible," Penny says. "People sent this magazine that
showed her body in the car with the blood and bullet holes. They called
her a white whore and a nigger lover, and said that she was having relations with black men."

Viola Liuzzo with her first husband, George
Argyris. This image was widely distributed
after her murder.

Even Sally Liuzzo, Penny's six-year-old sister, did not escape the public's wrath. Students threw rocks at her and taunted her on the way to school, Penny says.

The family was even more devastated to learn who had initiated the public backlash—J. Edgar Hoover, director of the FBI. To absolve itself of culpability in her death—an FBI informant was in the car with the men who killed Liuzzo—the FBI released her psychiatric records and directed a smear campaign to suggest that Liuzzo was promiscuous.

"Your mother has not died in vain," Reverend Martin Luther King Jr. told Penny at her mother's funeral. Yet she wondered for years if that was true.

The loss of her mother and the public backlash shattered Penny's family. Her father never recovered. Her sisters and brothers struggled. And Penny carried around a knot of bitterness for years.

The effect on Sally, her youngest sister, was brutal. "My heart just broke when Sally was eleven years old and we went to visit my mom's grave and she just sobbed on my shoulder, 'Please, tell me what she was like. I don't remember. I don't remember. Please, I can't remember her voice.'"

But Penny still has plenty of memories of her mother. She was the eldest child and spent the most time with her. Today she is a mother herself, a housewife living near Fresno, California, with her boyfriend, Bryce, and four sons. She is a warm and open woman who loves to laugh. It's odd to connect a string of tragedies with such a cheerful woman. Now fifty-six, she has struggled with diabetes and was once legally blind until laser surgery helped her see well enough to drive. She still talks at schools to keep her mother's memory alive. "She was always for the underdog," she says of her mother. "Once our neighbors had a fire. She went around and took up a collection to replace the toys—this was around Christmas time—they had eight kids."

Mary Stanton, author of the definitive Liuzzo biography, *From Selma to Sorrow*, says that Liuzzo once discovered that a secretary at her job was laid off without severance pay. She gave the woman her entire paycheck hoping it would embarrass their employer into giving the woman severance. It didn't, and Liuzzo paid for her activism by losing her own job.

Viola Liuzzo was a restless person. She married at sixteen but annulled it the next day. She married again and had two daughters, Penny and Evangeline (also called Mary); seven years later she was divorced again. In 1950, she married Anthony Liuzzo Sr., a Teamsters leader. They had three children, Anthony Jr., Thomas, and Sally.

She was also ambitious. Viola Liuzzo wouldn't settle for being a housewife. Though she was a ninth-grade dropout, in 1961 she enrolled in night classes to become a medical assistant. She graduated with top honors. She was a member of the Catholic Church but left after a priest told her that a child she had miscarried would never see the face of God. She joined the Unitarian Universalist Church.

Stanton says she was intrigued by Liuzzo's refusal to play the part of the submissive housewife. While her neighbors were taking cooking classes or doing church volunteer work, Liuzzo was preparing for a career, crusading for workplace rights, and going back to college. "She was one of these people who got really involved in everything she did," Stanton says. "They become like a vortex that sucks other people into their enthusiasm."

Penny Liuzzo, fifth from right, with family during requiem mass for her mother, Viola Liuzzo, at the Immaculate Heart of Mary Church in Detroit on March 30, 1965. Right to left: Jim Liuzzo, Tommy Liuzzo, Barry Johnson (Mary Liuzzo's husband), Mary, Penny, Sally Liuzzo, and Tony Liuzzo.

By 1965, Penny was becoming closer to her mom after some stormy adolescent years. "I just graduated from high school and we had just become friends," she says.

When Liuzzo decided to go to Selma, she did it in typically impulsive fashion. She was taking classes at Wayne State University when she called home. "I'm going," she cheerfully announced. "I'm on the way."

That's when Penny had her premonition. She tried to persuade her mother not to go, telling her that she would die. "I'll pee on your grave," Liuzzo told her daughter, laughing. And off to Selma she drove.

There, Liuzzo was one of 2,000 marchers gathered in response to a plea from King. She plunged right in, joining the movement's transportation committee, ferrying civil rights marchers around Selma for six days. Some of those marchers were black men. Liuzzo had to be aware of the dangers of a white woman being caught in the car with a black man at the time, says David Truskoff, one of the Selma marchers who met Liuzzo in Selma.

Truskoff, who would later write *The Second Civil War*, says Reverend James Reeb had just been murdered when Liuzzo arrived in Selma. Cars displaying swastikas drove by marchers constantly. White locals made obscene gestures at white women marchers walking next to black men.

The journalists who had assembled for the Selma march weren't that much better, Truskoff says. The press trucks that covered the Selma march were "half-full of rednecks." Many of them had heard Governor Wallace publicly warn Alabamans that white women like Liuzzo who had come down from the North for the march would be going back home to give birth to black babies.

Truskoff says he warned the marchers that these journalists were trying to photograph marchers at night when they camped out in the open during the five-day, fifty-mile march to Montgomery. "What some of these crackers really wanted to see were black men with white women in some of these sleeping bags."

The last time Truskoff saw Liuzzo was in a Selma church. She was standing before an applauding audience with a check in her hand. "She brought it up onto the stage and gave Hosea [Williams] a check from her husband's union," he says. "On her way back there was a big cheer and applause. She was just beaming. She walked past me, nodding at me as if to say, we're going to win this thing."

On the last day of the march, Liuzzo joined the 3,200 people walking into Montgomery for a rousing rally capped by a speech by Reverend King. She then drove back to Selma with Moton and other marchers.

Liuzzo dropped off her passengers in Selma and returned with Moton to Montgomery to pick up more marchers. They were driving on Highway 80 when a car filled with four white men pulled alongside Liuzzo's car. One of the men shot Liuzzo in the head, killing her instantly, according to police reports.

President Johnson appeared on television the next day to announce the arrest of four Ku Klux Klan members: Eugene Thomas, forty-three; William Eaton, forty-one; Collie Leroy Wilkins Jr., twenty-one; and Thomas Rowe Jr., thirty-four. Rowe, it was later disclosed, was an FBI informant.

The condemnation of Reverend Reeb's murder in Selma had been instantaneous and widespread. That was far from the case for Liuzzo. Racism, sexism, and the FBI combined to provoke a backlash against her.

First, an all-white, all-male jury acquitted all four men of Liuzzo's murder. Then they were tried again under different charges. Their trial was moved to a different jurisdiction and three were sentenced to ten years in prison for violating Liuzzo's civil rights. The fourth, Rowe, was not convicted after being granted immunity.

After the verdict, Stanton says, bumper stickers started appearing on cars and trucks in Lowndes County, where Liuzzo was murdered, saying, "Open Season."

The FBI then went after Liuzzo's reputation. Stanton says they tried to cover up for the fact that their informant in the car did nothing to prevent Liuzzo's murder. Hoover began telling President Johnson that Liuzzo was having sex with black men, was a drug addict, and had a husband who was involved in organized crime. The FBI then leaked this misinformation to the press, which soon began writing stories questioning Liuzzo's mental health (she had once suffered a nervous breakdown) and her morality. Anthony Liuzzo found himself defending his wife's character before newspaper reporters. The Liuzzo family would only discover what the FBI had done years later, after obtaining documents under the Freedom of Information Act.

Penny says her father was eaten away by the criticism of his wife. "It took the soul right out of him," she says. "He never was the same. He started drinking a lot."

Stanton says Anthony Liuzzo Sr. was viewed as a failure. "He was seen as a macho teamster who couldn't keep his woman in line." He died in 1978, still tormented about the gossip surrounding Viola. For a decade he had been trying to persuade the FBI to return her wedding ring to him. They finally did so—two years after he died.

The effect on the other family members also was devastating. Penny had two bad marriages; so did Sally. Penny says both married too quickly as a way of taking their minds off the loss of their mother. Sally was hit particularly hard by the death of her mother and, later, her father. "Sally has just got a grip on her life and she's in her forties," Penny says. "She was an orphan at twenty." (Mary, who is also called Evangeline, is a successful executive, however.)

Her two brothers, Tony and Tommy, who were thirteen and ten at the time, later dropped out of high school. "They were devastated and they retreated from society," she says.

Anthony Liuzzo Jr., the eldest son, has periodically popped into public view since his mother's murder. In 1975, he filed a $2 million lawsuit against the FBI on behalf of himself and his siblings for the agency's complicity in his mother's death. "My brother always said there was a government conspiracy, but I didn't believe him," she says.

During the trial, the FBI admitted that it had shredded 10,000 pages of documents connected to Liuzzo's murder. Still, the FBI won. In 1983 a federal judge threw out the lawsuit and ordered the family to pay the government $80,000 in court costs. The judge later changed that demand after the television show 20/20 did a report on the trial and people became outraged at the judge's order.

Penny says she was shocked to learn about the FBI's role in her mother's death. "At first, I thought they were the heroes," she says quietly. "I was disappointed. I didn't want it to be that way . . . I wanted America to be like our forefathers wanted it to be, and it's not."

The court's decision changed the lives of her brothers as well, she says. "It drove my brothers nuts," she says. "They couldn't take it anymore."

Today, Anthony Jr. is a leader in a militia faction and believes the U.S. government set up Oklahoma City bomber Timothy McVeigh. Penny declines to talk in detail about his life. But stories that appeared in the *Detroit Free Press* and *The Boston Globe* show a man on the fringes of society, living in a trailer in the backwoods of central Michigan, carrying a .45-caliber pistol in a shoulder harness at all times, and broadcasting a radio show about government conspiracies and the new world order.

The stories portray a man who, along with his wife, is stockpiling food and arming himself for an imminent revolution. But Anthony Jr. says he isn't bitter over his mother anymore. He has forgiven all four of the killers. "Yahweh has a plan for me," he told one Associated Press reporter. "I am not bitter. . . . I am doing my mother's work." He says he, too, is battling to uphold the Constitution. "I felt very strongly my mother gave her life for this country. I am willing to do the same."

But Anthony Jr. doesn't talk publicly anymore, Penny says. "Ever since 9/11, he's gone way underground."

After her mother's death, Penny, too, felt as if she were being dragged into despair with the rest of her family. Once, when Penny was

Courtesy of Valica Boudry

Anthony Liuzzo Jr., Viola Liuzzo's eldest son, living underground as a militia leader today. After he learned about the FBI's role in his mother's death, Liuzzo developed a deep distrust of federal government.

in a college political science class, she interrupted an instructor who was talking about justice in the South, telling him, "There is no justice in the South."

The teacher knew who Penny's mother was. "Every dog has its day," he told her.

Penny wondered if that were true, especially after her family lost the suit against the FBI and was forced to pay the court costs.

Katie Rager, Penny's longtime friend, says Penny was simmering with anger when they became friends. "She was angry at the government. She was angry at the KKK. We would just talk for hours and hours about how unfair it was, about how the people who murdered her mother took her away from her kids."

Penny admits that her mother's death made her pessimistic about her own future. "I prayed every night, 'God, don't take me away from my kids. Don't let me die until my kids are older.'"

She found some refuge in her faith. With Rager, she used to go to a little church near Fresno and read Bible verses about forgiveness. She began reading about Native American spirituality, which emphasized being grateful for every little thing in life.

Rager says that Penny gradually changed—so much so that whenever Rager had a problem, she turned to Penny. "She came out of this cocoon of loathing, hate, and anger and just blossomed into this beautiful, empathetic person."

The bitterness may subside, but not Penny's sense of loss. Over the years, Penny says, she found herself dreaming about her mother. She misses her spark and energy. "Sometimes when I'm feeling blue, I wish I could call my mother up."

She has never been tempted to blame God for her mother's murder. "You can't blame the Higher Power for what man's free will does. We all have our paths to go down. She chose that path and God loved her. He must have."

Another way Penny was able to overcome bitterness was thinking of her mother's attitude toward hate. Liuzzo had seen much of it growing up in the segregated South. "My mom said the best thing, and I took it to heart: 'Hate hurts the hater, not the hated. It eats you up. It's too consuming. It makes you so unhappy.'"

Motherhood gave Penny another reason not to be bitter. When Penny gave birth to her first son she resolved not to let her anger infect her boys as it had the other men in her family. "How can you be a good mom and be hateful?" she says. "Adults who grow up prejudiced—how did they learn that? Their parents were role models. You have to be a living example."

Penny got her chance to be a living example with an unexpected encounter in court. During her family's suit against the government, Penny was giving a deposition when she encountered Eugene Thomas, one of the men arrested for the murder of her mother.

Penny was sitting outside the courtroom in a waiting room with her son, John, when Thomas walked into the room. At first, he just stood there and said nothing as he looked at her, Penny says. Then he asked her, "Can you forgive me?"

Penny paused. Then she said, "Yeah, I do."

Thomas' shoulders relaxed and relief seemed to wash over his face. "Thank you," he said. Then he turned and walked out of the room.

After she tells me that story, I ask Penny why she would so readily forgive the man who participated in the killing of her mother. Penny says she actually felt sorry for Thomas. He looked like he was in agony. "I didn't hesitate. I could see the look on his face. I'm not out to crush people. Everybody lives with their own torture."

She didn't hesitate because she's now found something else to live for—her sons. Penny says she doesn't want to hurt anymore. So she's chosen to be grateful, not bitter. It's what her mother would have wanted. "I really have a good life. I'm not the richest person in the world. But I have people who love and adore me. All four of my boys, I've never had a major problem with my kids. If God would say I'm going to grant you a gift for my life, I would never have come up with the gift he gave me."

Ben Chaney and Angela Lewis
Brother and daughter of James Earl Chaney

BEN CHANEY SLUMPED TO THE GROUND and covered his eyes to cry.

As a cluster of photographers circled him to snap his picture, the twelve-year-old began to cry so hard that his thin body shuddered. People walked up to him to offer comfort, but he shooed them away. He finally rested his head on the right shoulder of his mother, Fannie Lee.

That was the first time most people would see Ben, the younger brother of James Earl Chaney, one of three civil rights workers murdered in Mississippi during the summer of 1964.

He was then known as "Little Ben Chaney." In the pictures news photographers took of him at his brother's memorial service, his resemblance to his brother was uncanny: the same almond-shaped eyes, high forehead, and oval-shaped lips.

The last time Ben saw his brother alive was on a Sunday morning. James Earl Chaney, often called J.E., had stopped by with his friend and colleague, Michael "Mickey" Schwerner, for some homemade biscuits. Both were going to investigate a church burning and Ben wanted to go.

"No," James Earl Chaney told his little brother. "We'll be back later."

Ben sat on his front porch that afternoon and waited for his brother to return. He waited into the evening. He waited so long that his mother finally ordered him to bed.

He would wait forty-four more days before he discovered what had happened to his older brother. James Earl Chaney had been ambushed and murdered along with Schwerner and another civil rights volunteer, Andrew Goodman.

The murders became international news. Photos of "Little Ben Chaney," shattered by grief at his brother's memorial service, would make their way across the world.

But few people know what happened afterward to the grieving boy in the photos. Few know about the anger that followed Ben's tears; the murder spree that claimed the lives of three white people; his thirteen years in prison; and his eventual return to Mississippi to seek justice for his brother.

Few knew that when Ben collapsed into his mother's arms and wept that morning, his pain was just beginning.

Ben Chaney trudges through the snow in a wind-swept cemetery in Meridian, Mississippi, until he finally reaches the place. He stands on a desolate hilltop before a marble headstone printed with the name "James Earl Chaney."

At the top of the headstone is a small picture of the deceased. But as Ben leans forward to look at the picture, his eyes narrow: two bullet holes pierce his brother's image.

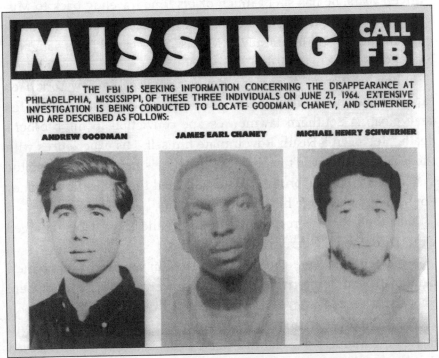

The chilling "missing" poster that was distributed by the FBI after James Earl Chaney disappeared in Mississippi along with fellow civil rights workers Michael Schwerner and Andrew Goodman.

Ben traces the bullet holes with his right index finger. "This is the fourth or fifth time the grave has been desecrated," he says. "Before, there were attempts to open up the vault to get to the coffin."

⸺⠶⠶⠶⸺

This is the first time I've met Ben. I've been assigned by a newspaper to meet him in Mississippi to talk about his brother. But he acts nothing like the sensitive twelve-year-old who allowed the entire world to witness his grief. The fifty-year-old man who stands before me is stoic, wary; his face betrays no emotion as he looks at his brother's bullet-pocked headstone.

Perhaps Ben needs all the emotional reserve he can get. For the past thirteen years, he has spent much of his time traveling back to Mississippi to campaign for the retrial of the men accused in his brother's murder. He also still has family in Mississippi—James Earl's daughter, born a week after his murder.

When he's not in Mississippi, Ben is a paralegal in New York. He's experienced almost every angle of the legal system imaginable. He's seen gloating Southern lawmen escape conviction in his brother's death. He's been a Death Row inmate himself. His experiences with the legal system haven't been good, but Ben is now trying to use the system to avenge his brother. He established the James Earl Chaney Foundation to preserve his brother's memory, but he wants more.

Ben wants the men responsible for his brother's death to be charged with murder. But he is running out of time.

Nineteen men were eventually arrested in the deaths of Chaney, Goodman, and Schwerner. Two of them were Mississippi lawmen: Sheriff Lawrence Rainey and Deputy Sheriff Cecil Price.

A Ku Klux Klan member confessed to FBI agents that he had witnessed the murders. He claimed that Price had arrested and released the three civil rights workers that night, knowing that a mob was waiting to ambush them on a rural road. But despite this and another confession, no Southern jury would ever convict anyone for the actual murder of Chaney or his colleagues.

Fannie Lee Chaney and her son, Ben, on the front porch
of their home in Meridian on August 5, 1964, right after
they learned that James Earl's body had been found
and identified near Philadelphia, Mississippi.

In 1967 prosecutors managed to convict eight of the men for conspiring to deny the civil rights of Chaney, Schwerner, and Goodman.
None served more than ten years. Some of those originally arrested,
including Lawrence Rainey and Cecil Price, have recently died—Price
fell from a cherry picker and Rainey died of throat cancer.

Ben believes that the state of Mississippi is hoping that the rest of
the men will die so that it won't have to endure the ugly publicity of a
new murder trial. He has personally reviewed the 2,900 pages of tran-
scripts from the trial and even the autopsy photographs (he says his
brother was beaten so badly before he was shot to death that it looked
as if he had been in an airplane crash).

When he talks about his brother's murder, Ben never brings up the
possibility of forgiving the men who were arrested in his brother's
death. He says about twelve of them are still alive. Though they are old,
he wants them tried again.

I ask him if he's still angry after all these years. "I don't know if I'm
angry at them as individuals or as a group," he says. "But I know that
I'm angry over the fact that my brother is dead and no one has been
brought to justice for his death."

He has no interest in trying to discern the mindset of the men who killed his brother. He doubts if any of them experienced any guilt or regret during the years that have followed. "They feel the way they felt back in the 1960s," he says. "They felt justified in what they were doing, and they still feel justified."

Ben says his brother had no illusions about the men he was going against. He knew they would kill. But he persisted because there was this tremendous frustration building up among blacks in Mississippi by the early 1960s. "A lot of young African American males in their teens and early twenties were looking for an opportunity to do something. When the opportunity came, a lot of them didn't do anything, but a few did."

James Earl Chaney didn't wait long to plunge into the movement. A native of Meridian, he was once suspended from high school for wearing an NAACP badge. In 1963 he began working in the Meridian office of the Congress on Racial Equality (CORE).

In the summer of 1964 Mississippi Freedom Summer began. Young black civil rights workers in groups such as Student Nonviolent Coordinating Committee (SNCC) and CORE invited hundreds of white college students to come to Mississippi to help them register black voters. James Earl Chaney joined in.

Ben says history books and photos don't do justice to his brother's personality. The infamous poster circulated after the three civil rights workers were missing shows Chaney staring at the camera with a stoic, almost glazed, look on his face. But Ben says that his brother was a practical joker who liked to gather with his friends on the corner to sing Motown. He was asthmatic, but he managed to become the captain of his high school football and track teams. As he talks about his brother, Ben's voice softens and his sense of humor bubbles to the surface. He still has his Southern accent.

Ben also has vivid memories of Schwerner, his brother's murdered colleague. Schwerner had become a family friend through frequent visits. He was a chubby guy who loved baseball and nicknamed James "the bear" and Ben "the cub." "The one thing I remember about Schwerner

Ben Chaney weeps at the funeral service for his brother, James Earl Chaney, in Meridian, Mississippi. On Ben's left are his father, Ben Chaney Sr., and his mother, Mrs. Fannie Lee Chaney.

is that if you were in a room with him and he was talking and you didn't know he was white, you would swear he was black," Ben says.

Ben rode often with his older brother and Schwerner. It was fun, and he felt safe with his brother. They took him to demonstrations and Ben was even arrested twice. But his brother sensed that people were out to get him. "I think he was aware of the danger," Ben says. "He had been out many other times before. He had driven at high speeds with no lights on, running from Cecil Price on back dirt roads. He knew what would happen if they got caught."

When searchers eventually found his brother's body buried in an earthen dam, Ben says he still refused to accept that his brother was dead. Then it hit him at the memorial service and all his grief came pouring out. "It wasn't until early that day at the burial that I realized that, hey, this was final," he says. "That's when death became real to me."

Then Ben began to receive other reminders that life was fragile. His family started receiving death threats over the phone. Their house became the object of random gunshots and firebombing. Some people weren't satisfied that his brother was dead.

Finally Fannie Lee Chaney moved Ben and her three daughters to New York for their safety. Carolyn Goodman, the mother of Andrew Goodman, helped set the Chaney family up.

Goodman designated Ben as the first recipient of the Andrew Goodman Memorial Scholarship at the Walden School, an alternative private school where Goodman had once been a student. Ben was one of twenty-five black students in a student body of about eight hundred. He was living in a big city for the first time. "It was like going to a foreign land," he says.

But Ben never found his footing at Walden. He stayed there for five years but admitted he was an indifferent student. He would often skip school to seek his education in Harlem. "When I first went to Harlem, it was like heaven," he says. "Black people were in control. The streets were clean. The music, poetry readings—Harlem, brother, was it."

It was the late 1960s and black nationalist movements were seizing the imagination of young black people. Nonviolence seemed naive to them. Groups such as the Black Panthers talked about black power and using violence if necessary to defend their communities.

The message resonated with Ben, who was now a young man. "There was a period where I felt like I hated mankind," he says. "I wanted to vent my hatred and my anger on white folks. To me, they were the main perpetrators for evil in the world."

Ben became an activist like his brother. But it was different now: no nonviolent struggle. In late 1969, he and other activists took over a YWCA because it refused to install a Black Panther Party free breakfast program for children. He even organized one demonstration in New York that ended in a riot. He spoke around Harlem about the need for black people to train themselves in self-defense. Some people, though, questioned his black revolutionary credentials because he had been educated at a white school.

James Sullivan, another black high school student, met Ben during that time. Now a computer consultant in New York, Sullivan chuckles at the figure Ben cut when he started going around New York in his dashiki and sandals to tell black students to get organized. "He was a string bean, a bowlegged country bumpkin. He walked like he just got off a horse. He had that real, slow, Southern demeanor, definitely not New York."

But Ben never talked about his brother's murder to his friends. Sullivan says he only found out about it through others. When Sullivan brought it up, Ben didn't elaborate. "It took us so long to realize who he was. There was never any celebrity about it. It was a fact of life for him."

Despite his brother's death, Ben didn't seem to be driven by rage. "I never saw him yell or raise his voice," Sullivan says. "He had this under-the-surface intensity. It was a smoldering intensity. It was like, we need to get things done."

Ben says he didn't become an activist just to avenge his brother's death. Like many people, he thought a black revolution was imminent and he wanted to participate.

He got his chance and paid dearly for it.

In April 1970, one of Ben's friends asked him to accompany him while he visited a relative in Florida. On the way there, the man told Ben the trip's true purpose: they would be picking up a shipment of guns in Florida to transport them to a Black Liberation Army unit in Ohio.

What happened next sent Ben to prison. Three white people were shot to death and two wounded during a murder spree that crossed Fort Lauderdale, Palm Beach, and South Carolina. At the age of eighteen, Ben was sentenced to three consecutive life terms for the murder of a white insurance salesman and two college students.

Ben maintains that the charge was not justified. "I never killed anyone," he says calmly. "I was charged and convicted primarily because I would not tell after the acts were committed—I didn't know the acts were going to be committed ahead of time. I did not go and tell the cops that this person had killed someone."

Ben spent the prime of his life—thirteen years—in prison. While there, he discovered that his last name both helped and hurt him.

Ben Chaney is photographed in Philadelphia, Mississippi, on June 20, 1999, while visiting the state to prod Mississippi prosecutors who, he says, have "more than enough evidence" to bring his brother's killers to justice.

Black prisoners respected and protected him because of his brother's death. They knew he was coming before he actually arrived in prison. But prison officials tried to break him psychologically because of his name. He says he spent two years in solitary confinement because he questioned a white correctional officer about an order to cut his hair.

Prison, he says, transformed him. He got his AA degree in prison and later got his BA degree from John Jay College. He was a clerk in the prison library where he consumed books such as Malcolm X's autobiography, George Orwell's *Animal Farm*, and various biographies.

Most of all, prison taught him patience, he says. "You spend a lot of time in line waiting. You gotta stand up in the morning and line up for the count. You gotta line up to go to breakfast, lunch, and dinner. You gotta line up and wait for mail. You gotta line up to do anything."

Ben's name helped him win support on the outside. His mother, declaring that she would not lose another son, organized a letter-writing campaign to the parole board. The famous attorney William Kunstler filed his case with the Supreme Court, which refused to hear it.

In 1983 former U.S. attorney general Ramsey Clark finally interceded and persuaded the Florida parole board to release Ben. When he was released, Ben immediately flew to New York, where he remains today.

Sullivan says Ben still has a sense of mission. His office, where Ben frequently works well into the evening, is filled with books and articles on black America and the prison system. "Even to this day, I get calls from him about ideas he wants to try out. If I don't move fast enough, he's already moved on. I don't think he can sit still. He has to be constantly doing something."

Despite their lifetime friendship, Sullivan says they have never talked about Ben's slain brother or his time in prison. "I guess it's a thing guys just don't talk about."

But Ben keeps close to Mississippi. In 1989 he established the James Earl Chaney Foundation to stop vandalism of his brother's grave. Four years later, he returned to Mississippi to help in an investigation into the suspicious deaths of several young black men found dead in Mississippi jail cells. He has another reason for going back: his brother's daughter, now thirty-eight, lives in Meridian. Angela Lewis, a nurse, has four kids and is married to a police officer.

Angela was born out of wedlock, a week after her father was murdered. She says she didn't know how her father died until she was about thirteen years old. Before and since that time, her mother has never talked about her father.

Nor does her grandmother talk about her father's death much. "My grandmother is still hurt," she says. "If you speak with her, you would sense that my father's death just happened yesterday."

When she discovered how her father died, Angela says she didn't experience any anger or deep sadness. She couldn't miss someone she never knew. "My reading about him today is like reading about a stranger."

She remembers reading about her father in high school history class. But she would never say a word about who she was. She didn't want the attention. It was only when she became a mother that she really missed her father. "I didn't realize what I missed until I saw my daughter with her daddy," she says. "Just to hear her calling him dad and know how he's always there for her—that's the only time I had that sense of longing."

A devout Christian woman who sings in her church choir, Angela talks easily about her loss. She says she even occasionally saw the man accused of murdering her father, former Sheriff Lawrence Rainey. He was a security guard at a mall near her home.

She says she never was tempted to say anything to him. "I don't think he ever changed," she says. "I don't think a conversation would have changed him. From what I heard, he still referred to us as niggers."

Angela says she doesn't hate the men who murdered her father. She thinks somehow they will pay—in this life or the one to come. "What happened to my dad was because of hate," she says. "For me to live in hate would be to carry on the very thing that took him out of the world."

Ben says he has changed, too. He no longer hates white people. He was baptized eight years ago and is the father of a sixteen-year-old girl, Amelia. "I'm an old man now," he says ruefully. "The time for violence is pretty much past. It's not a viable tool. Black people aren't prepared for the consequences. We're too entrenched in this system. We have to look for ways to make the system work for us."

That system, however, still has not worked for Ben.

He's no longer the twelve-year-old boy sitting on the front porch waiting for his big brother. He's a man now. But four decades after his older brother was beaten and shot to death on a deserted Mississippi road, no one has been convicted for his murder.

Ben is still waiting.

Anne Reeb
Daughter of Reverend James Reeb

ANNE REEB REFUSES TO PLAY THE PART that fate has assigned her. She won't call her father a hero. She is not on a mission to bring his killers to justice. She doesn't choke up when talking about his death.

Anne is the daughter of Reverend James Reeb, one of the movement's most honored martyrs. When Reeb was murdered during the Selma campaign in 1965, his death ignited a series of events that led to the greatest victory of the civil rights movement.

President Lyndon Johnson went on national television to lament the young minister's death. Tributes to Reeb poured in to his family; the tributes continue thirty-nine years later. One Wisconsin church named its congregation after Reeb. Busts and murals of his image are spread throughout the nation.

But Reeb's daughter won't participate in the canonization of her father. She says she has watched her father become transformed into a hero for reasons he would have detested; her father's death is universally mourned because he was white. "A week before my father died, Jimmy Lee Jackson [a black activist] was killed, but the media didn't take hold of that loss of his life," she says. "They didn't put that on the front page of every newspaper. The president didn't come on the phone and call his family."

Anne once felt so conflicted about the attention that has been paid to her father's death that she personally apologized to relatives of Jimmy Lee Jackson. It's something her father would have wanted her to do, she says. "My father would not like to say that he was a hero, because Jimmie Lee Jackson was a hero. Many other people, who were unnoticed and unaccounted for, gave their lives."

Anne, forty-two, is immersed in a profession that has little to do with the grim event that shook her childhood. She operates a circus. The cofounder of a theatrical group, Earth Circus, in San Francisco, and a professional dancer and stiltwalker, she orchestrates the performances of puppeteers, jugglers, and clowns for educational and corporate events. "It's a lot of fun," says Anne, who is married with two children. "You're telling stories. We're kind of like kids who never wanted to grow up."

One story she doesn't like to tell concerns the death of her father. When I talked to the daughter of Viola Liuzzo or the brother of James Earl Chaney, both seemed to exude a sense of duty when talking about their loss. They wanted people to remember. But Anne, a laconic woman, downplays any drama associated with her father.

For example, I ask her how it felt for her to go back to the street corner in Selma where her father was murdered. "There was sadness," is her nonchalant response. No elaboration. And then she moves on to talk about the bleak economic conditions of Selma.

Perhaps Anne doesn't offer much detail about her father because her memories are so few, so fragmented, and so painful. At the time of her father's death, she and her four siblings were living in a black neighborhood in Boston. Her father was working for the American Friends Service Committee, also known as the Quakers.

Then Reverend Martin Luther King Jr. issued a call to clergy of all faiths to come to Selma to demonstrate for black voting rights.

"When he answered the call, my father was working in the inner city trying to get better housing for the black community," she says. "Therefore, instead of living in a white neighborhood and going into a black neighborhood and saying this is what we need to do to get better housing, he moved his family into the same kind of housing."

The portrait of Reeb that was distributed after his death shows a man who looked like a young Orville Redenbacher—clean-shaven, bow-tied, short hair neatly parted. That, undoubtedly, was part of the reason his death struck so many Americans deeply. They could see themselves in him.

But those who knew the minister say that he was far more complicated than the wholesome image his photo suggested.

Reeb was born into privilege. The only child of a corporate executive, he grew up in an all-white community in Casper, Wyoming. But

Reverend James Reeb. His death was so galvanizing to the
Selma movement that a mural of his image still hangs in
the town today.

as early as high school, he empathized with blacks and poor people—
he volunteered at a Boys' Club to help Casper's poorest youth.

He felt called to the ministry as a young man. He attended Prince-
ton Theological Seminary and worked as a hospital chaplain after grad-
uation. But he wasn't fulfilled by traditional religion. He became a
humanist, someone who believes that religion should be based on
rational thought and tolerance, according to his friend and biographer,
Jack Mendelsohn.

Reeb eventually left the Presbyterian Church and became a Unitarian, a creedless religion that emphasizes social activism. He became an associate minister at one of the largest Unitarian churches in the country, All Souls in Washington, D.C.

"He could have become the senior minister of a major congregation if he wanted," Mendelsohn says. "He would have risen to prominence."

Reeb gave up that job, however, to take one that paid much less, and he moved his family into a black neighborhood. According to Mendelsohn, he wanted to live alongside the people he was helping.

While applying for the Boston job, Reeb wrote: "Many Negroes are living in . . . wretched conditions. They see few white people that are interested in their welfare."

Reeb had a habit of surprising people, recalls Reverend Orloff Miller, a Unitarian Universalist minister who was with him at the time of his murder. Miller still remembers the first time he met Reeb at All Souls. "Jim was seated with his feet on his desk, smoking a cigar, and chatting on the phone—then and there shattering any preconceptions I might have had of this ex-Presbyterian."

On Reeb's desk was a copy of a prayer that gave a clue to his spiritual worldview: "Grant us peace fearlessly to contend against evil and to make no peace with oppression, and, that we may reverently use our freedom, help us to employ it in the maintenance of justice among men and nations."

"He had a wonderful positive attitude," Mendelsohn says. "Even though there was injustice he had this very hopeful approach that you could do something about it."

With that attitude, no one was surprised when Reverend Reeb accepted King's plea for clergy to come to Selma.

Mendelsohn, who was the pastor of the Unitarian church that Reeb attended at the time, says Reeb's wife, Marie, didn't want him to go. But he felt he had to. The last evening he spent with his family, Reeb tucked his children into bed, read them bedtime stories, and kissed his wife goodbye.

He was on his way to Selma.

The young minister walked into a battle zone. The "Bloody Sunday" march at the Edmund Pettus Bridge had already taken place. And at least 2,000 marchers, including 450 clergy, had come from around the country to march again.

One evening at dusk, Reeb met two ministers, Reverend Miller and Reverend Olsen, for dinner at Walker's Café in downtown Selma. Miller remembers it as a peaceful, warm spring evening. After eating, they phoned their wives to let them know they were OK. Then they set off for a nearby church.

The three walked alongside one another; Reeb was closest to the curb. Suddenly three white men began shouting at them, "Hey, you niggers!" They quickly came up behind the group.

Olsen remembers himself and his two companions saying to one another, "Just keep walking. Just keep walking."

Then one of the Selma men took a club and hit Reeb behind the left ear. He crumpled to the ground. There was no blood, but Olsen could tell his friend was in bad shape. "He was babbling," Olsen says. "He was holding his head and he was just incoherent. We knew that something terrible had happened to his head."

The young minister's skull was fractured. The two men picked him up and carried him to a nearby black infirmary for help. Olsen says Reeb tried to communicate as he lay in the infirmary. "I was holding Jim's hand and Jim squeezed my hand tighter and tighter, apparently from the pain," Olsen says. "And then he went unconscious."

They called an ambulance and accompanied the injured minister on a harrowing three-hour journey to a Birmingham hospital, delayed by a flat tire and trailed by a carload of local whites.

Two days later, Reverend Reeb died. He left behind his wife and four children.

When he heard that his friend had been injured, Reverend Mendelsohn rushed to the Reebs' house in Boston to comfort Marie. For two days, he and Marie received updates from the hospital. When the radio reported her husband's death, at first she looked stunned and said nothing. Eventually, she broke down, Mendelsohn says.

She then asked Mendelsohn to break the news to her eldest child, thirteen-year-old John. She wanted to tell her three youngest children herself. Mendolsohn says the image of John Reeb reacting to the news of his father's murder is burned into his memory. After he sat him down in the kitchen and told him the news, a mixture of bewilderment, pain, pride, and resolve flashed across the boy's face. Then he cried. "He cried a good deal, and then he stiffened up, squared his shoulder. My impression was that he was deciding that he was the man of the family and that he was going to get grown up in a hurry."

Anne says her mother woke her up in the morning to tell her. She was five years old at the time. "I just remember her saying that my father had been hurt and that he was in Selma and that he had been hurt badly enough so that he wasn't coming home," she says. She didn't know what it meant. "I actually thought that someday he would return," she says. "I thought he was just hurt."

The reaction to the minister's death was instantaneous. Thousands demonstrated across the nation and groups of clergy demanded action. President Johnson sent a military plane to move the Reeb family from Boston to Casper, Wyoming. The murder also led to an epoch-shifting event for the civil rights movement. President Johnson used the dramatic leverage from the event to urge the U.S. Congress to pass the Voting Rights Act, which swept away the barriers Southern whites had erected to prevent blacks from voting since the end of Reconstruction. Within a decade, the number of black elected politicians in the South went from 72 to 2,568.

But vindication eluded the Reeb family in a Southern courtroom. Three men were arrested and charged in the attack. All three were tried and acquitted by an all-white, all-male jury, though, as Mendolsohn recounted in *The Martyrs*, both Olsen and Miller positively identified one of them during the trial.

Anne says she wasn't angry at her father's killers. She was angry she didn't have a father to play with. "There were a lot of my friends who were having activities with their dads. You could see how a family was complete with the mother and father. There were times I was very angry at that."

She says her brother, John, lost faith in organized religion because of what happened to their father. "He was angry as a twelve-year-old with God," she says. "I think he's still pissed. He was angry at God for taking his father away. It's affected his beliefs in terms of a higher power. He has a hard time talking about it now."

Anne says she sometimes tried to convince herself that her father was still alive. "I would have dreams that he would show up at our house one day. That stuck in my mind. Even though later I realized that he actually died." Her mother made up for her father's absence. "My mom was such a strong woman. She was a big enough presence to carry our family through. She was both mom and dad."

Anne's mother enrolled her in gymnastics, tap, and ballet classes. She attended the University of Utah, where she earned a degree in modern dance and theater. She then moved to San Francisco, where she formed Earth Circus in 1990.

Her father had tried to reach people through his faith. She tries to do the same through her art. Her circus has educated people about preserving the environment and HIV awareness. Now it primarily does corporate events. "People can latch onto it [a message] if it's creatively presented," she says. "It takes them out of being preached to. Politics can get a little dreary. If it's presented in a way with color, parade, theater, dance, and poetry, they'll listen."

What some people may find hard to latch onto is the fate of the men accused of killing James Reeb. Only one of the three is still alive. His name is O'Neal "Duck" Hoggle; he runs a restaurant and a used car business near downtown Selma. Most of his customers are black.

Many people are shocked to learn that a man who was tried for the killing of Reverend Reeb is making a good living in Selma today. Local activists and the Southern Christian Leadership Conference (SCLC) tried to organize a boycott of Hoggle's business, but it failed.

Joanne Bland, a Selma activist who works at the National Voting Rights Museum, says blacks patronize Hoggle's car business because he's the only business that finances cars for people with bad credit. When she and others tried to get customers to stay away, they weren't interested. "When you're poor and oppressed, sometimes it's easier to say, that happened before my time and I don't know anything about it. So they say, 'Why am I going to punish this man that looks like he's giving me a helping hand by letting me get a good car when I have very little money?' "

Hoggle's acceptance infuriates Olsen. He returned to Selma in 1998 with his daughter, Marika, a television producer who filmed a documentary for CNN about his return to Selma. CNN obtained the FBI's file on Reeb's murder, and according to CNN, the file reveals that eyewitnesses saw Hoggle attack Reeb. Olsen personally obtained the same file a year later; reading it reinforced his conviction that Hoggle was part of the group that attacked Reeb.

Olsen says he's been tempted to try to talk to Hoggle himself. He resents the fact that Hoggle is living well. "I think I would ask him, 'What have you done with yourself now?' How has he thought about it? How has he reconciled himself? If he is a person who goes to church or believes in God, how does he put this together? And what has he done in any way to make up for the terrible deed he did?"

Anne had her chance to meet Hoggle when she returned to Selma in 1990 on the twenty-fifth anniversary of the Selma march. She even walked down the alley in downtown Selma where her father was attacked. Her mother, who accompanied her, refused to even get out of the car. The memories were too painful.

Meeting Hoggle with her mother there was out of the question, she says. "That would have traumatized her if I did it. I think that's a bit dangerous in a way."

A friend traveling with Anne asked a passerby what had happened in Selma during 1965.

The man, oblivious as to who Anne was, said Selma was "a mess." "He said all these people were coming into Selma who shouldn't be here," Anne recalls. "He said, 'There was this white minister who got killed. He shouldn't have been poking his nose around here and stirring up trouble.' "

Anne says the man's comment didn't make her angry. She was angry at times over the absence of her father, but she never thought much about the men who were tried in connection with his murder. Losing her father at such a young age may have dampened her anger. "When you're younger, the information that you get around the reason why your father isn't there is a little bit fuzzy. The reasons aren't as clear as they are when you become an adult."

As an adult, Anne talked herself out of any anger toward the men who killed her father. She said her father's killers were shaped by what they learned growing up and where they lived. "You can rationalize everything as an adult," she says. "That's how I was able to handle it. I didn't personalize it."

Anne did have one meeting with figures from her father's past that stays with her today. When she attended a dedication ceremony for a civil rights memorial in Alabama, she met relatives of Jimmy Lee Jackson. She apologized to them for the silence that greeted Jackson's death because he was black. One of Jackson's relatives hugged her.

Shirley Robinson, a cousin of Jackson's, says her family holds no bitterness toward Reeb's family for the attention his death received. "He was trying to do the same thing Jimmy was," Robinson says of Reeb. "We don't have any remorse. We understand that at the time, we knew that he wasn't going to get much publicity being black."

What hurts Jackson's relatives more is that no one was ever arrested in connection with his death. And when a memorial to Jackson was erected in Marion, Alabama, vandals shot bullet holes into it.

Jackson's mother, Viola, doesn't like to talk about the murder to this day. Jimmy Lee Jackson was her only son. "We have to learn how to forgive and go on," Robinson says.

And that's what Anne has done today.

So what does she call her father, if not a hero, I asked her?

She uses the same description that President Johnson used when he went on national television to talk about her father. "I would say he was a good man," she says. "He wanted to make a difference in the world. He just didn't want to talk about it. He wanted to be out there doing it."

7

The New Radicals

From Selma to Seattle

IN DECEMBER 1999 AT LEAST 40,000 demonstrators laid
siege to and eventually shut down a meeting of the World
Trade Organization (WTO) in Seattle, stunning the American public. The coalition of groups included aging activists
such as consumer advocate Ralph Nader and Tom Hayden,
the former California senator who founded the Students for
a Democratic Society (SDS). But most of the marchers were
American college students battling riot police and tear gas in
what seemed like a replay of the 1960s.

The Seattle protest is now regarded as a pivotal moment
in the global justice movement. Like the Montgomery Bus
Boycott of 1955, it signaled the start of a new mass movement. Since Seattle, global justice protests have drawn huge
crowds in cities all across the United States, South America,
and Europe. And terms such as *globalization* and *privatization* have made their way into everyday speech.

The global justice movement is not the sole arena for
activism today. Civil rights groups such as the NAACP
remain vital, and thousands of anonymous civil rights workers continue to do crucial work. But the protestors from

Seattle represent the biggest and most dramatic mass move-ment for a new generation of activists.

Defining this movement, though, is tricky. Like the civil rights movement, it includes many different factions. It fea-tures animal-rights activists, anarchists, and students against sweatshops—pick a cause and you'll find it there. But the movement is, at its essence, a battle against corporate greed on an international scale. A new generation of radicals believes that corporations are now more powerful than gov-ernments. Their enemies are more elusive—no swaggering, brutal Southern sheriffs like Eugene "Bull" Connor—but anonymous bureaucrats and corporate leaders.

Leaders in the global justice movement say, though, that their movement didn't start with Seattle. "There's nothing original or new that happened in Seattle; it was a wake-up call for the people in the mainstream media that have been ignoring the resistance to corporate globalization," says Andrew Dellinger, one of the people profiled in this chapter. "All of the work we're doing is building on decades of resist-ance in places like India and Nigeria."

Many of these new radicals also say that their work is built on the civil rights movement. Not surprisingly, the parents of some of the leaders in the global justice movement par-ticipated in the civil rights and antiwar movements. These leaders cite their parents, along with Martin Luther King Jr. and the student sit-in leaders, as their inspiration.

Some may question the links between Seattle and the civil rights movement. Yet the truth is that the civil rights movement was never just about overturning Jim Crow. By 1968 King had already come out against the Vietnam War and was about to launch a Poor People's Campaign to force America to confront its poverty. Just five months before he was assassinated, King predicted that a battle centered on the "economic colonialism" of the world's poor would be the next chapter of the movement. "It is clear to me that the next stage of the movement is to become international," he said in a sermon aired by the Canadian Broadcasting Corporation. "National movements within the developed countries—forces that focus on London, or Paris, or Washington, or Ottawa—must help to make it politically feasible for their governments to undertake the kind of massive aid that the developing countries need if they are to break the chains of poverty. We in the West must bear in mind that the poor countries are poor primarily because we have exploited them through political or economic colonialism."

The final chapter of this book shows that the movement is ongoing, albeit in a new incarnation. Three new radicals talk about the links between their parents' civil rights activism and the movement today. It's a new century, they say, but the distance from Selma to Seattle is not as far as one might think.

———∞∞∞———

Andrew "Drew" Dellinger
Son of Walter Dellinger

ANDREW KING DELLINGER LOCKED ARMS with his friends and moved into the intersection as tear gas swirled and mounted police surged toward them. He should have been afraid, but tears of joy welled up in his eyes.

Drew was surrounded by 40,000 demonstrators who were banging cowbells, dancing, and singing. Spoken-word artists rapped from the tops of vans mounted with speakers. Environmentalists dressed in turtle shells marched in columns. The festive street scene was filled with American college students, Amazonian tribesmen, and middle-aged steelworkers, all grasping hands together.

It was the first massive global justice protest in the United States. Demonstrators had flooded Seattle to shut down a meeting of the WTO. Thirty-two-year-old Drew was part of a group that used "lock-boxes," or plastic tubes, to lock their arms together as they staged a sit-in the middle of an intersection. Earlier, they had met outside downtown in a "convergence space"—a place thousands of demonstrators passed through to don costumes and receive medical and legal training.

The protest also represented another kind of convergence for Drew. He is the son of Walter Dellinger, a progressive Southern lawyer who picketed a segregated movie theater in his youth and worked on behalf of the civil rights movement by becoming a Constitutional law scholar. His father was so inspired by the movement that he gave Drew the middle name "King."

But for much of Drew's life he couldn't find another mass movement for social justice. Instead, he found his inspiration in the past. He became a spoken-word poet and taught a class on the sit-in movement and the early civil rights movement at Prescott College in Arizona.

Then he heard about the Seattle protests. Eventually, he was arrested along with 500 other demonstrators in Seattle and spent three days in jail. But he returned to the protests and has since become a leader in the global justice movement in the United States.

Courtesy of AP/Wide World Photos

Animal protection advocates wear sea turtle costumes while carrying signs to protest what they contend are animal-harming rulings by the WTO in Seattle on November 29, 1999. Drew Dellinger plunged into the center of these historic protests, which shut down the WTO after thousands of protestors flooded downtown Seattle.

"I felt like I was able to take a stand for justice that I've been waiting all my life to take," he says of the Seattle protests. "It was a glorious feeling to be out on the street and to see the spirit of celebration, to see the empowerment in people's faces."

James Zwerg, the Freedom Rider whose assault at the hands of a white mob was captured in an unforgettable photograph (see page 26), once lamented that he could never recapture the euphoria he had experienced in the movement. If he had been in Seattle, he might have felt it again.

When I talk to Drew, I think, this is what it must have been like for a journalist to interview college students who were leading sit-ins or joining freedom rides in the early 1960s. They exude the same sense of passion and idealism, the belief that what they're doing will literally change the world.

But there are differences between the movements that Drew, a student of civil rights history, likes to point out. There is a similar commitment to massive nonviolent protests, engaging young people, and attacking the causes of poverty. But global justice protestors have also pioneered new protest tactics for the twenty-first century.

One difference is how they craft their public image. Being media savvy is nothing new for any activist. Civil rights leaders were masters of using the media. The Black Panthers, for example, knew the symbolic power of placing young black men in leather jackets and giving them shotguns. The protestors in Birmingham exploited the images of police dogs attacking demonstrators to gain sympathy. But the festive images of protestors in Seattle seemed to convey something new.

There were no solemn marches framed by grim-faced leaders dressed like undertakers. The protests in Seattle looked like a mobile rave party. People danced, rapped, built massive puppets, and dressed in whimsical costumes (one of Drew's enduring images of Seattle is of protestors dressed as Wonder Woman and Superman).

Drew says the atmosphere was planned. Protestors wanted to give people a sample of the world they wanted to live in. "The idea was to revitalize the culture of protest using the powers of art. It's the art of celebration. It draws a stark contrast to the cold and sterile world of the corporate mentality where we build these gray concrete cities where every worker goes to their cubicle."

They also created new props to get media attention. The use, for example, of giant puppets lumbering down the streets was designed for a new generation of people with remote controls and short attention spans. "Puppets make these incredible visual images that can be seen from far away," Drew says. "What do you think is going to make the front page—more people standing on the corner holding placards or a big, beautiful, giant puppet that says global justice on it? It encapsulates the message if you're trying to reach people who have five seconds to glance above the fold."

The global justice protests even *sound* different from the civil rights movement. The black church provided the soundtrack for much of the civil rights movement with freedom songs such as "Eyes on the Prize." Blacks also furnish much of the musical inspiration for the global justice movement, but the sound doesn't come from the rural black church tradition. The music carries the thumping beat and percussive rhymes of hip-hop. Drew, who lives in Berkeley, California, uses spoken-word poetry and rap music to talk about globalization. His presentations are heavily influenced by artists like KRS-One and Public Enemy. Several of his poems and essays have appeared in books about the global justice movement and its new leaders.

Drew says groups like Public Enemy inspired him to write lyrics that deal with issues such as environmental justice and corporate fraud. In his poems, Drew attacks his subjects with the ferocity of a rapper. He mixes braggadocio with borrowed advertising jargon (one poem uses the refrain, "Attention, shoppers! Freedom is no longer cost effective!"), exhorting his fellow protestors with a bullhorn at global justice events.

Rap lyrics reach people in a way that speeches and books cannot, he says. "The arts are captivating. They speak to people's emotions. They impact people on the deepest level."

Drew Dellinger performing his spoken-word poetry at a protest for global justice.

Like his predecessors, Drew has learned that protest doesn't pay well. He's worked as a tutor and delivered pizza to get by. He makes some money through his poetry performances and by teaching at Prescott College, where he's a graduate student studying world religions. "The rewards are a lot deeper than the financial rewards," he says. "I work with some of the most amazing and inspiring people on the planet."

Yet most of them are white. While many leaders in the global justice movement cite black leaders in the civil rights movement as inspiration, very few blacks appear at any of the protests. "White people don't drop their racism the minute they start working for justice," Drew says. "The continuing racism in the global justice movement is one of its biggest stumbling blocks."

Drew says the racism is so subtle that most whites aren't aware they harbor such feelings. But their language betrays their condescending attitude toward blacks. "A lot of people say, 'How can we get people of color into "our movement,'" as opposed to 'How can I support the leadership and struggles that activists of color are already in?' "

As a white male, Drew says he feels a "burden" to confront racism—even when it may touch himself. "We live in a nation founded on white supremacy," he says. "Though my ancestors may not have been in this country when certain events unfolded, as a white person, I inherit hundreds of years of privilege."

Growing up in the South as the son of liberal parents also shapes Drew's views on race. His father, Walter Dellinger, worked with the NAACP Legal Defense Fund, taught Constitutional law at the University of Mississippi, and later became acting solicitor general under President Clinton. He argued nine cases before the U.S. Supreme Court. Dellinger's mother is Anne Maxwell Dellinger, a law professor at the University of North Carolina.

His father also knew what it felt like to be excluded. According to an article he wrote for Duke Law School magazine, Walter Dellinger was raised as a Catholic in the predominately Protestant South during the 1940s and 1950s. He was also inspired by the *Brown v. Board of Education* decision, which he saw as "a shining example of the law's awesome redemptive power," the article says.

When reached at his home in Chapel Hill, Walter Dellinger confirms the importance of the Brown decision in the formation of his thinking. Growing up in the segregated South, he took for granted that the races should be separated in the classroom. "The very existence of Brown turned it from a question of fact into a moral question. If you had asked me when I was in the sixth grade, the year before *Brown*, whether I thought segregation was right or wrong, I don't think I would have understood the question. It was like asking whether it was right or wrong that the moon came out. Brown made it wrong and put the moral question to the country."

Walter Dellinger picketed a segregated movie theater when he was a student at UNC-Chapel Hill in 1963 but says he had little of the sophistication of Drew's generation. He's gone to hear his son's

Walter Dellinger, Drew's father. Walter
admires his son's work but disagrees with
him about the effects of globalization.

performance poetry and came away impressed. "There was none of
that when I was growing up," he says. "The best we had were completely inept rhymes on picket signs that said, 'Skip this show so that
all may go.'"

Despite the middle name he gave his son, Walter Dellinger says he
really doesn't know where his son got his racial sensitivity from. "He
had black friends from the earliest time—by the time he was in the
fourth or fifth grade. There comes a time when the races separate when
they move into the higher grades, but that was never true of Andrew.
One of Andrew's best friends is an African American kid he met in his
kindergarten class."

Drew says his father's work as a civil rights attorney shaped him.
Through his father's example and his own study, he came to believe that

the links between the civil rights movement and the antiglobalization movement are "palpable." He decided to get involved in more direct forms of action after reading about the exploits of young people in the movement who formed the Student Nonviolent Coordinating Committee (SNCC) and became Freedom Riders. That decision led him to the streets of Seattle. "I like to tell today's activists the story of how a spontaneous action by four students at Greensboro A&T sparked the sit-in movement that grew to include 50,000 people within three months," he says.

Seattle has sparked something similar—another mass movement to capture a new generation of activists. "Sometimes a single rock triggers a landslide," Drew says. "I nourish my hope with this image from the civil rights movement."

Naomi Klein
Daughter of Bonnie Sherr Klein and Michael Klein

EVERY SUCCESSFUL MASS MOVEMENT has to have one.

One had a young Baptist minister who electrified a crowd at the Lincoln Memorial one day while telling them about his dream.

Another had an unemployed Polish electrician who formed a labor union that ultimately defeated the Communist Party in Poland.

And who can forget that mysterious man who blocked the path of Chinese tanks during the Tiananmen Square protests?

That one is the person who, through word or deed, makes a movement come alive to the masses. In the global justice movement, that person is Naomi Klein, a thirty-two-year-old Canadian born to American parents who were active in the civil rights movement.

Klein isn't giving speeches or manning the barricades. She's made her impact with a groundbreaking book, *No Logo*. Dubbed "the *Das Kapital* of the growing anticorporate movement," it came out at a time when most people in the West were unaware that a global movement against corporate domination even existed. Yet Klein boldly predicted that the next major political movement would be an international coalition of activists targeting multinational corporations. The Seattle protests, which took place shortly after her book was released, validated her claims.

Books lamenting big business's exploitation of the world's poor had come out before, but two things made Klein's book different. First, it was accessible. She used humor, pop culture references, and autobiography to explain the global justice movement to ordinary readers. After reading her book, people began to look at the global reach of companies such as Nike and McDonald's in a new way.

The other distinctive feature of *No Logo* was Klein herself. She wasn't a tweed-wearing academic or ranting anarchist. The critic of runaway consumerism was a twenty-something former mall rat who had been so obsessed with brand names that she used to stitch fake alligators on her T-shirts so they would look like Lacoste polo shirts. She fought constantly with her activist-parents who thought she was too frivolous, a claim that she and her youthful friends embraced.

"We wanted to be Valley girls," Klein told me. "We were intensely proud of being superficial. We were one of the first generations to see hanging out at the mall as a major activity."

But as a teenager Klein experienced a crisis that ignited her activism. Today, her parents are still stunned by how that event changed their daughter. "This was a kid who didn't feel strongly about anything besides clothes," her mother, Bonnie Sherr Klein, says from her home in Montreal.

Courtesy of Michael Klein

Naomi Klein before she wore name brands. The Klein family, from left to right: Seth Klein, Bonnie Sherr Klein, Michael Klein, and Naomi Klein.

"It was a sudden metamorphosis," says her father, Michael Klein.

That metamorphosis culminated in the writing of *No Logo*. When it was released in early 1999, the excitement over globalization had reached its peak. Communism was dead. Capitalism had triumphed. The widespread belief, reflected in commercials such as IBM's long-running "Solutions for a Small Planet" campaign, was that multinational corporations would bring the world together.

Klein described the mood in the beginning of her book: "Usually, reports about this global web of logos and products are couched in the euphoric marketing rhetoric of the global village, an incredible place where tribal people in remote rainforests tap away on laptop computers, Sicilian grandmothers conduct E-business, and 'global teens' share, to borrow a phrase from a Levi's Web site, 'a worldwide style culture,'" she wrote.

Brands were the symbols of this triumphant global economy. She called them the "closest thing we have to an international language." The Nike swoosh, the McDonald's arch—each is recognized by most of the world's population.

What Klein showed, though, was the human misery that goes into producing these brands. She was one of the first to talk about issues such as Nike's sweatshops in poor countries. "The travels of Nike sneakers have been traced back to the child laborers of Sumatra, Starbucks' lattes to the sun-scorched coffee fields of Guatemala, and Shell's oil back to the polluted and impoverished villages of the Niger Delta," she wrote.

Klein says that brand names had become so pervasive that they were infiltrating public school cafeterias, movie house intermissions, the sides of buildings—people couldn't get away from them. The result: a backlash against corporate rule that helped spark the global justice movement.

Then Klein, writing before the massive protests that would take place in Seattle later that year, made a prediction: "As more people discover the brand-name secrets of the global logo web, their outrage will fuel the next big political movement, a vast wave of opposition squarely

Courtesy of Michael Klein

Naomi Klein, as a young girl, with her father, Michael.
Their relationship would become strained when Naomi
became a teenager who shunned her family's activist
tradition.

targeting transnational corporations, particularly those with very high name-brand recognition."

The prediction seemed outlandish at a time when the global economy was booming. This was years before Enron and the economic collapse of Latin American countries such as Argentina. "There was a real sense that anybody who had bad news about the global economy and wanted to talk about anything that was behind the wealth and boom was not really welcome," Klein says today. "It was like talking about death at a wedding."

Klein's gravitation to protest politics is part of her family's tradition. Her grandparents were Marxists in the 1930s. Her grandfather, an animator for Disney (Donald Duck), was fired after organizing a strike.

As she talked about her upbringing, Klein laughed aloud at the incongruity of growing up in a household where she had parents who criticized her for *not* being radical enough. Both of her parents were shaped by three progressive movements that sprouted during the 1960s: the civil rights, antiwar, and feminist movements.

Her father moved to Canada with her mother after he was drafted. An antiwar protester, he refused to serve in Vietnam. Her mother was a member of the Congress of Racial Equality (CORE) and participated in sit-ins during the late 1950s. Bonnie Klein is best known today as a feminist and an award-winning filmmaker; her antipornography film, *Not a Love Story: A Film about Pornography*, brought her a measure of fame.

Growing up in Montreal, Naomi and her older brother, Seth, were exposed to left-wing causes. Her parents played eight-track tapes of civil rights and labor union songs. Her mother's first film was about Cesar Chavez and migrant workers. They attended a liberal, Reconstructionist synagogue where social activism was encouraged. "The story of activism is a part of the folklore of the family," says Michael Klein, now an internationally known doctor who lives in Vancouver.

Yet Naomi was ambivalent about following in the family tradition. Her mother had received a lot of attention for making her film about pornography. Then her brother, Seth, got a lot of media attention when he became an antinuclear activist and traveled around Canada to visit students. "He took to it, I didn't," Naomi says. Her father is more blunt: "His sister thought he was a dork."

Naomi recalls one moment in particular when her mother took her to an antinuclear protest in New York. She was ten years old at the time. "I became conscious that I was kind of a prop. I said to my mother, 'I'm never coming to another protest.' "

Conflict at home followed. Naomi, in particular, battled with her father during her teenage years. He'd grown up in a frugal household with parents who were marked by their experiences in the Great Depression. She says he found the idea of a kid getting a new bike repulsive. He couldn't understand her preoccupation with clothes and designer labels. "He would ask what was I doing after school and I would say, 'I'm going to hang out at the mall,' " Naomi says. "He would just flip out and say, 'What does that mean to go to a mall and just hang out?' I would tell him, 'You'd rather I deal drugs than hang out in the mall?' "

Courtesy of Michael Klein

Naomi Klein as a young girl.

Whenever the subject of politics or responsibility came up, his daughter tuned him out, Michael Klein says. "She hated it. She thought I was shoving stuff down her throat. Naomi reacted by becoming a mall rat."

The schools Naomi attended fueled her resistance. At one, in an affluent section of Montreal, the subject matter was "cars and clothes." Her friends couldn't understand her mother's films and her brother's peace activism. "I would just be sneering at them with my friends so that people would know that I wasn't like them," Naomi says. "I was a popular kid in school and I was just interested in clothes and boys, fitting in, and people thinking that I was pretty."

Yet her parents wanted her to carry on the family's tradition of activism. They didn't understand the pressures of a teenage girl trying to fit in. "I didn't know how to reconcile the 1980s with what was going on in my house," she says.

The other part of her rebellion was rooted in her personality. "I am a natural-born rebel," she says. "I didn't like being told what to do. My parents were authoritarian about their hippieness."

Naomi's willingness to defy authority, though, would become instrumental in launching her writing career. She first discovered that she could blend her skills as a communicator and her family's tradition of protest during her Bat Mitzvah speech. She chose to talk about the racism in her school, where many Jewish kids made fun of Moroccan Jews who attended a school next door. "She got a standing ovation for the speech," her father says. "The rabbi published her speech in the synagogue bulletin."

It was at that moment that Naomi discovered that she could distinguish herself by something other than the brand names she wore. "I was very proud of it," she says of the speech. "But at the same time I remember being so concerned about how I looked: what was I going to wear and thinking that I was fat."

Yet the event that had the most impact on her was when, as she was preparing to attend the University of Toronto to study English and philosophy, her mother had two severe strokes. At one point Bonnie Klein was put on a respirator. She became confined to a wheelchair. Naomi took a year off from college to care for her. Her brother, Seth, was away from home.

Naomi says the stroke erased the tension she experienced with her father. "We had to work together. It was just the two of us. We had to make peace."

Michael Klein says his wife's stroke forced Naomi to jettison whatever animosity she had toward him. "Naomi lost her struggle with me and overnight became a close friend and ally. She supported Bonnie in the most incredible way."

Courtesy of Michael Klein

Naomi Klein, in sunglasses, with family today. Klein's husband, Avi Lewis, on left; her mother, Bonnie, in the middle; and her father, Michael, on far right.

Bonnie Klein says her daughter went from a "bratty troublemaker" to her rock. "Any brush with death is a call to basics, and the love-hate relationship with parents—you don't have much room for the hate. There was a role reversal. I needed her desperately."

After her mother's condition stabilized, Naomi dropped out of college. She drifted into journalism, working as an intern at the Toronto *Globe and Mail* and becoming the editor of an alternative political magazine in the early 1990s.

It was during this time that Naomi first became disenchanted with the Left. In an interview with the *Guardian* of London, she said the Left seemed exhausted. "The only thing left-wing voices were saying was stop the cuts, stop the world we want to get off. It was very negative and regressive. It wasn't imaginative. It didn't have its own sense of itself in any way."

Worse, Naomi added, was the way that multinational corporations cannibalized the progressive language of the Left—diversity, racial justice, feminism—to sell products using celebrity pitchmen such as Tiger Woods ("There are still courses in the United States where I am not allowed to play because of the color of my skin"). At the same time that Nike was portraying itself as a leader in the campaign against racism it was forcing thousands of people of color to work on starvation wages in sweatshops in Southeast Asia. But it was difficult to see this relationship with the focus on the brand. "Nike also realized that people who saw themselves as belonging to oppressed groups were ready-made market niches: throw a few liberal platitudes their way and, presto, you're not just a product but an ally in the struggle," she wrote in *No Logo*.

Naomi knew she wasn't the only one who saw this contradiction. She began to notice a new generation of activists who were targeting multinational corporations such as Nike. She began to believe that a significant movement was building and she wanted to capture its energy. She decided to write *No Logo*.

"She told me this was going to be a bestseller and it was going to change the world," her father says.

When the book appeared in 1999, it seemed to put in words what so many people had been feeling. It has gone on to become a bestseller. Naomi is now a spokesperson for a new generation of activists. She has lectured in Europe and North and South America about *No Logo*.

Naomi says she has seen the public skepticism of corporate greed grow after the Enron and WorldCom scandals. "What's being questioned now is how wealth is accumulated—not the labor conditions for a particular factory, but whether you can trust American capitalism. That's a huge leap forward."

Naomi currently lives with her husband in Argentina, where she is filming a documentary about that country's attempt to build a new form of democracy since its economy collapsed.

Her father says he was stunned when he finally read his daughter's book. He had never seen her write with such authority. "We don't even understand how the hell she acquired her political sophistication."

Naomi says it was there all along. Even when she was entranced by the mall, she had never abandoned her family's tradition. She read, she wrote, she noticed how people were suffering around her. Her Jewish identity has always made her sensitive to social justice issues. She read voraciously about the Holocaust as a young girl. She saw her parents' involvement in the civil rights movement as an extension of their Jewish heritage. "When I heard, 'Never again,' that meant that you would fight any kind of discrimination," she says. "That was part of being Jewish. Part of being Jewish is fighting for someone who is persecuted."

As she gains more popularity, though, more journalists are depicting her as a soulless mall rat who was transformed by a cataclysmic event. Even when she was obsessed with finding the trendiest brand label, Naomi knew she wasn't going to remain at the mall forever. "I cared all along," she says. "But I was just messed up. As I became more confident in myself, a lot of the superficiality that came with trying to fit in went away. I grew up."

Timi Gerson
Daughter of Bill Gerson

AT THE AGE OF FIVE, TIMI GERSON was marching her Ken and Barbie dolls around her bedroom chanting, "Reagan, Reagan, he's no good. Send him back to Hollywood." At the age of eight, she was marching with her mother in demonstrations, carrying balloons that read, "Boycott South Africa, not Nicaragua." And as a teenager, she attended summer camps for the children of civil rights activists and labor organizers, where she sang "We Shall Overcome."

"I grew up knowing who Che Guevara was before I knew who George Washington was," Timi says.

Today, Timi is an organizer at Public Citizen's Global Trade Watch, a Washington, D.C.-based group that promotes corporate accountability in the globalization arena. The group was one of the members of the coalition that flocked to Seattle in 1999.

Timi says the global justice cause is trying to show people a new form of oppression that's just as evil as anything seen during the civil rights movement. "A corporation that makes more money than the combined GNP of half of the African continent is just as morally wrong as separate water fountains."

Timi didn't just discover radical politics when the Seattle protests hit the news. She was already primed for the movement. During the 1970s and 1980s, when street protests were seen as a relic of the 1960s, she and other children of civil rights activists were quietly being trained to carry on their parents' activism through a network of mentors and summer camps.

Twenty-seven-year-old Timi is the daughter of Bill Gerson, a former leader in Students for a Democratic Society (SDS) and an antiwar protestor. Her mother, Carol Higgs, organized opposition to the Ku Klux Klan and the American oppression of Latin American countries. Her

A young Timi Gerson with her father, Bill, at a demonstration. She was so immersed in demonstrations as a young girl that she played with her dolls by making them demonstrate.

grandmother was a union organizer, and her grandfather was editor of the Marxist newspaper, *The Daily Worker*.

Bill Gerson says he sent his daughter to summer camps at the World Fellowship Center in New Hampshire, where she not only learned about the civil and labor rights movement, but she also learned self-confidence. "Kids from the Left or from progressive families sometimes feel isolated. Their parents are called the eccentric ones and their parents are the ones who go to demonstrations and do weird things. When they go to places like the World Fellowship Center it gives them a chance to see that there are plenty of people like them."

Part of Timi's current job is to explain the global justice movement to the public. She leads teach-ins across the United States and in South America (she's fluent in Spanish) on subjects such as globalization, debt restructuring, and participatory budgets.

She doesn't have an easy sell. The massive demonstrations in places such as Seattle may seem bewildering to the average American, but in Timi's view, they're concerned with the same issues that drove civil rights activists to register black voters in the South during the early 1960s.

"It's about democracy," she tells me from her home in suburban Maryland. "Fifty-one of the hundred largest economies aren't countries, they're corporations. But corporations aren't accountable to anybody. You can say they're accountable to their shareholders or to their consumers. But really, they're not accountable like my congressman in my district is accountable to me."

Neither are the groups that set the rules for these multinational corporations, which often smooth the way for the latter to prey upon poorer countries. International agencies such as the WTO and the International Monetary Fund (IMF) routinely meet in secret to agree on how to regulate and interact with one another. "These secret agreements are often shaped by business lobby groups and are unrelated to anything that citizens voted for," she says. "These institutions are fundamentally undemocratic."

One of the challenges of the global justice movement is making its goals clear to the public. Photographs of separate water fountains are easy to interpret. But how do you mobilize masses of people around abstract economic issues such as debt restructuring or the privatization of water rights?

"Abstract to whom?" is Timi's quick reply. She then points to the collapse of the Argentinean economy, which took place after it embraced economic measures imposed by the WTO and the U.S. government. "It's not abstract to Argentineans," she says. "The whole country is out on the street banging pots and pans. It's not abstract to steelworkers who've worked in the same factory for forty years and just got laid off. It's not abstract to the kid who gets poisoned by a corporation's bad environmental practices."

Timi says these issues are only abstract for middle-class Americans who are shielded from the ravages of global poverty. Yet she senses that in the post-Enron world, many Americans are growing uneasy about the growing power of multinational corporations. She believes that the time will come when most Americans will be able to understand the perils of globalization, just as they now understand the importance of the environment due to the work of environmentalists. "An environmentalist was considered totally left-wing crazy in the 1970s, and now I don't think you can find anyone under fifty who couldn't talk knowledgeably about global warming and recycling or the importance of sustainable environmental policies."

As Timi speaks about these issues, her passion is palpable. She talks at a turbo-charged pace, firing off numbers, quotes, and long bursts of opinion. She also has a quick sense of humor and frequently makes fun of her upbringing.

A native of Annapolis, Maryland, Timi jokingly says she was raised in a crazy "commie" family. Her father was a "red diaper baby," child of communists. When her grandmother, a Russian Jewish immigrant, was nineteen, she hitchhiked from Massachusetts to North Carolina to help lead a 1929 mill strike.

Timi grew up in a household where protest was part of the family routine. She accompanied her mother to weekend demonstrations. She grew up singing along to labor classics such as Woody Guthrie's "The Union Maid" ("There once was a union maid, she never was afraid of goons and ginks and company finks and the deputy sheriffs who made the raid . . .").

"When Timi was younger, she thought the song was about her grandmother," Bill Gerson says.

Timi's grandmother, Sophie Melvin, was one of her first heroes. She grew up hearing how her grandmother had led the mill strike, a dangerous business in the South during the 1920s. In fact, a deputy sheriff was killed during the mill strike and Timi's grandmother was tried for murder (the newspapers of the time referred to her as the "beautiful Red Sophie Melvin," Timi says) but later acquitted. "She's been an incredible inspiration. Whenever I talk to people about why I'm doing what I'm doing, I always tell her story. She is the person I measure myself against."

Protest wasn't seen as a 1960s fad. It was part of a long tradition that extended back to Marxism. "My parents used to always say that we were not hippies or liberals; we were radicals," Timi says. "In their opinion, liberals whined about things and radicals did something about it."

Carol Higgs, Timi's mother, says she routinely took her daughter to meetings and demonstrations because she couldn't afford a babysitter. She also broadened her daughter's outlook by carefully screening the books she gave her as a child. In the fairy tales her daughter read, the heroes were often women or people who came from other cultures.

"She had one book about a little boy who liked to wear a skirt," Higgs says. "All the children laughed at him but he didn't care because he was a strong kid. Those kinds of stories help children learn to be different. If you are different, people might talk about you, but that's because they don't understand that it's much more fun to be different."

The World Fellowship Center also helped Timi to accept being different. At the camp, she met people like her grandmother. Labor leaders, environmentalists, and political dissidents—they all came to talk to the kids. Camp leaders made sure the camps were integrated, and they gave scholarships to poor minorities. After the political lectures, Timi hiked, swam, and ate from the camp's organic garden with her friends.

Still, at times, Timi was reminded she was different. The first time it really hit her came when she was in the fifth grade, and she was listening to a teacher tell her class how the communists took over Cuba and would one day try to take over the United States.

What Timi knew about communists came from her grandparents. She heard that they believed in workers' rights and racial and gender equality. She decided to share her thoughts with her teacher. "I raised

Timi Gerson today, with her mother, Carol Higgs, at a demonstration. The global scope of her daughter's activism stuns Carol Higgs.

my hand and said, 'So what would be so bad about that?' She freaked out," Timi says, laughing at the memory.

Timi drifted into the global justice movement while attending Indiana'a Earlham College, a Quaker school. There, she joined a program that sent her to Colombia for two years. At the time, she defined herself as a feminist, but being exposed to widespread poverty convinced her that other issues such as inequality and lack of democracy were just as important.

Then the 1999 protests in Seattle took place. Timi was visiting Costa Rica at the time but she saw it on television and her mom sent her e-mail descriptions of the protest. Inspired and energized by the events in Seattle, she returned to the United States. Her reaction was one of relief. "Thank God the Left in my country finally has something to say," she says. "There was a place to put this analysis through what I got through my family. Before Seattle, I felt at loose ends about what to do. Seeing Seattle, it clicked. It helped me figure out where to put my energy."

Timi joined the Public Citizen's Global Trade Watch. Since then, she's become a citizen of the world, traveling to Brazil, Peru, Puerto Rico, and—perhaps to the horror of her fifth-grade teacher—Cuba.

Through her travels, Timi says she's seen that the 1999 protests in Seattle weren't the momentary expressions of a group of middle-class white kids in America but part of a worldwide movement. That was apparent when she went to one global justice conference in Brazil—more than 60,000 people attended. "You had people from India, Ghana—it was one of the most mind-boggling experiences I've ever had."

Like other global justice leaders, Timi says South America has become what the South used to be during the civil rights movement— the battleground for a burgeoning human rights movement.

Brazil has recently elected as president Luis Inacio "Lula" da Silva, a man born in poverty whose entire campaign was based around fighting globalization in his country. The country is also offering a more democratic form of governmental spending: "participatory budgets." Communities gather to vote where their resources will go. Budget decisions are no longer left to a group of politicians meeting in rooms and making decisions shaped by lobbyists.

Timi says candidates who mirror Lula's politics have been elected in countries as diverse as Argentina, Bolivia, and Ecuador. "Latin America is going through a huge transition."

Yet unlike the civil rights movement, the global justice movement is not built around charismatic leaders. "It's a movement built from the bottom up," she says. "It's built by indigenous people in the Amazon, by student leaders in Ghana, people like me in the United States. There are some guiding intellectuals and activists, but there's a huge emphasis on consensus, the fact that everyone can be a leader."

Despite the movement's complexity, Timi says its goals are simple. Poor people around the globe, she says, should have the right to water, education, and health care. No multinational corporation coming into their community should be able to take those rights away from them. "At base, we want the people who are most impacted by the decisions that are made to be the people making those decisions," she says. "We want fundamental democracy in the global economy."

Bill Gerson, now the chair of the math department at Prince George's Community College, looks on his daughter's work with a mix of admiration and concern. He says his colleagues in the SDS were more naive than his daughter's generation. "One of the problems with the SDS is there we were, a lot of middle-class kids," he says. "A lot of them expected that they would go out and march, demonstrate, and they would get what they wanted immediately."

Gerson also worries about his daughter on a more personal level. The life of an activist is hard. His mother, Timi's hero, spent time in jail before her acquittal. Other members of his family were jailed during the McCarthy era, and he himself was followed by FBI agents as a kid because his parents were communists.

"You want your kids to share your values and believe in all these progressive ideas, but at the same time, it's your kid, and you don't want her harmed or hurt," Bill Gerson says. "If your kid is going to be an activist, it places her at greater risk than if she lived a nice middle-class life."

Timi says risks are inevitable for those who want to improve people's lives. Recently, she went to see a movie about the civil rights era, and her companion remarked afterward that Jim Crow was destined to fall because it was immoral.

Timi's response would have made her grandmother—and any other activists who struggled in the civil rights movement—proud. "Bull," she told him. "Because something is morally wrong doesn't mean it's going to fall. That is not how it works. It works through struggle. It fell because people worked their tails off."

Index